God's Word, by Orpheus J. Heyward, is a truly illuminating composite of years of academic compilation. In my judgment, this work will become a required read among students of the sacred text. The book's scope of topical themes provides a healthy perspective of holistic biblical theology. By design the book highlights the veracity of God's revelation and inspiration for the power of our own illumination. In his own words, "God has spoken."

— **Dr. O. J. Shabazz**, Harlem Church of Christ, NYC

God's Word is a clear, faithful guide to the origins and nature of Scripture. It's a must-read for answers to key questions about the Bible and its interpretation, written with both sensitivity and conviction. Dr. Heyward is a seasoned pastor, an erudite scholar, and a dynamic teacher. This book is a well of wisdom for pastors, students, and laypeople alike!

— **Paul S. Cable, PhD**, Ethos Virtual School, Dean of Academics, Chair of Bible

Dr. Orpheus Heyward's *God's Word* is a meticulously written journey through the Bible that highlights the authenticity of God's Word for humanity through Christ. This work dissolves theological complexity down to practical simplicity and brings the reader to a biblical recognition of the power of both the Word of God and the voice of God.

— **Jamel Hamilton**, Minister, Mountain View Church of Christ

GOD'S WORD

THE INSPIRATION
AND AUTHORITY
OF SCRIPTURE

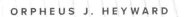

ORPHEUS J. HEYWARD

RENƎW.org

God's Word: The Inspiration and Authority of Scripture

ISBN (paperback) 978-1-949921-72-4
ISBN (Mobi) 978-1-949921-73-1
ISBN (ePub) 978-1-949921-74-8

Cover and interior design: Harrington Interactive Media (harringtoninteractive.com)

Printed in the United States of America

To my family. I am appreciative of the friendship of my wife, Sony. I am also grateful to my two vibrant children, Nevaeh and Nehemiah. Thank you for your support during this most difficult time.

CONTENTS

GENERAL EDITORS' NOTE

Theology for disciples of Jesus must come from Scripture. But studying Scripture leads to questions: What are the main themes of the Bible? What does it mean to say the Bible is "inspired"? And how did it come down to us in our day?

Orpheus J. Heyward is a helpful guide as we seek answers to these types of questions. He is the Senior Minister of the Renaissance Church of Christ. Having received his Master of Arts in Theology, Master of Arts in Biblical Studies, and Doctor of Ministry in Theological Exegesis, he is a constant student of the Bible.

This book expounds on the section from the Renew.org Leaders' Faith Statement called "God's Word":

> We believe God gave us the sixty-six books of the Bible to be received as the inspired, authoritative, and infallible Word of God for salvation and life.

The documents of Scripture come to us as diverse literary and historical writings. Despite their complexities, they can be understood, trusted, and followed. We want to do the hard work of wrestling to understand Scripture in order to obey God. We want to avoid the errors of interpreting Scripture through the sentimental lens of our feelings and opinions or through a complex re-interpretation of plain meanings so that the Bible says what our culture says. Ours is a time for both clear thinking and courage. Because the Holy Spirit inspired all sixty-six books, we honor Jesus' Lordship by submitting our lives to all that God has for us in them.

*See the full Network Faith Statements at the end of this book.

Support Scriptures: *Psalm 1; 119; Deuteronomy 4:1–6; Deuteronomy 6:1–9; 2 Chronicles 34; Nehemiah 8; Matthew 5:1–7:28; 15:6–9; John 12:44–50; Matthew 28:19; Acts 2:42; Acts 17:10–11; 2 Timothy 3:16–4:4; 1 Peter 1:20–21.*

The following tips might help you use this book more effectively (and the other books in the *Real Life Theology* series):

1. *Five questions, answers, and Scriptures.* We framed this book around five key questions with five short answers and five notable Scriptures. This format provides clarity, making it easier to commit crucial information to memory. This format also enables the books in the *Real Life Theology* series to support our catechism. Our catechism is a series of fixed questions and answers for instruction in church or home. In all, the series has fifty-two questions, answers, and key Scriptures. This particular book focuses on the five that are most pertinent to God's Word.

2. *Personal reflection.* At the end of each chapter are six reflection questions. Each chapter is short and intended for everyday people to read and then process. The questions help you to engage the specific teachings and, if you prefer, to journal your practical reflections.

3. *Discussion questions.* The reflection questions double as discussion-group questions. Even if you do not write down the answers, the questions can be used to stimulate group conversation.

4. *Summary videos.* You can find three to seven-minute video teachings that summarize the book, as well as

each chapter, at Renew.org. These short videos can function as standalone teachings. But for groups or group leaders using the book, they can also be used to launch discussion of the reading.

May God use this book to fuel faithful and effective disciple making in your life and church.

For King Jesus,
Bobby Harrington and Daniel McCoy
General Editors, *Real Life Theology* Series

INTRODUCTION

God has spoken. The author of the book of Hebrews writes, "In the past God spoke to our ancestors." But how did he speak? The writer continues by describing how God spoke: "through the prophets at many times and in various ways." Yet God didn't stop there. He then gave us his culminating Word: Jesus Christ: "But in these last days he has spoken to us by his Son" (Hebrews 1:1–2).

God has not left his people without the benefit of his voice. His words have long functioned as a guide to the people of God. His message finds climax in what Jesus spoke in these last days through his apostles. In this passage, the author of the book of Hebrews covers the spectrum of both old and new covenant history, declaring that God has provided his words in "the prophets" of long ago and in the person of Jesus.

The God who spoke throughout biblical-era history ensured that the spoken revelation would be written down. God's written Word of the Old Testament is often referred to in the Bible as "the Writings" (often translated "Scripture" or "the Scriptures"). In 2 Timothy 3:16–17, the apostle Paul provides a description of Scripture that gives insight into its nature:

> All Scripture is God-breathed and is useful for teaching, rebuking, correcting and training in righteousness, so that the servant of God may be thoroughly equipped for every good work.
> (2 Timothy 3:16–17)

The word that Paul uses for "inspired" (*theopneustos*) is an adjective that carries the meaning of God's *breathing* or *blowing*. The point is that God is the source of Scripture; it is "breathed out" by him. A look at the context of these verses shows that Paul has in mind the Old Testament

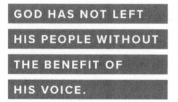

GOD HAS NOT LEFT HIS PEOPLE WITHOUT THE BENEFIT OF HIS VOICE.

Scriptures (2 Timothy 3:15). Yet there is reason to think that Paul would also see this description as applying to the full corpus of Scripture, including the New Testament writings. We see this through Paul's use of New Testament passages as he places them next to Old Testament passages and treats both as having equal authority. Notice, for example, in 1 Timothy 5:17–18 as Paul addresses the elders who labor in preaching and teaching:

> The elders who direct the affairs of the church well are worthy of double honor, especially those whose work is preaching and teaching. For Scripture says, "Do not muzzle an ox while it is treading out the grain," and "The worker deserves his wages." (1 Timothy 5:17–18)

In establishing the precedent that we should honor elders who labor in preaching and teaching, Paul provides two citations. The first reference is from Deuteronomy 25:4. The second reference is from Luke 10:7. This suggests that Paul believed that both Old and New Testament writings were "Scripture," thus treating both as authoritative.

The purpose of the book you're reading is to show how God's Word has been given by God, written by chosen writers under the guidance of the Holy Spirit, and that it teaches what we need to know for life and godliness. As Paul wrote in 2 Timothy 3:16–17, these inspired writings are beneficial for teaching, reproof, correction, and training in righteousness. Through the providential care of God, these Scriptures have been collected and preserved for perpetual use by God's people.

In the chapters that follow, I intend to lead you through a study of five questions that will focus on God's Word as sacred communication, which must be handled appropriately. These questions are:

1. What is the Old Testament?
2. What is the New Testament?
3. How did we get our Bible?
4. How do we interpret the Bible?
5. How is the Bible our final authority on what to believe and how to live?

May the answers to these fundamental questions encourage you to engage with biblical texts and gain more insight into God's Word and character.

We will look at how the Bible teaches us God's commands and covenants throughout history. Then, we will explore how the Bible came into existence, how it functions authoritatively for God's people, and how it should be responsibly interpreted so we can understand the meaning of God's communication. Although 2 Timothy 2:15 was written to a particular evangelist in a local church, the verse teaches us all how we should handle God's Word: "Be diligent to present yourself approved to God as a worker who does not need to be ashamed, accurately handling the word of truth" (NASB). To this worthy end, let's begin our exploration of God's Word.

1

WHAT IS THE OLD TESTAMENT?

Answer: The Old Testament is thirty-nine books containing God's promises, covenant laws, and guidance for ancient Israel throughout its history. It served as a tutor to lead Israel to recognize their need for a coming Messiah.

I will praise you with an upright heart
as I learn your righteous laws.
— Psalm 119:7

Throughout the years, people use the term "Old Testament" in two main ways: The content of the Old Testament books, and the old covenant as a governing law for Israel. For instance, consider this statement: "God commanded Israel to build the tabernacle in the Old Testament." And consider another statement, which uses the term the same way: "I read in the Old Testament how God brought Israel out of Egyptian bondage." When used in this first way, "Old Testament" means the content of the Old Testament books ranging from Genesis to Malachi.

Let's consider the second way in which "Old Testament" is sometimes used: the old covenant as a governing law. For example, you may have heard a person say, "Keeping the Sabbath is a part of the Old Testament," or, "'You should not covet' is a command in the Old Testament." When used this way, "Old Testament" can be a term referring to the content of the law that God gave when Israel met God at Mount Sinai. In this way, "Old Testament" is a synonym of "old covenant," the sacred promise God made with the Hebrew people at Mount Sinai. Both usages are accurate and proper when used appropriately.

It should also be noted that the phrase "Old Testament" is not a phrase used by the authors of Scripture. Christians first used it as a designation for the Hebrew Scriptures. The Hebrew Scriptures were traditionally divided by Jewish people into a twofold categorization of "Law and Prophets" (see Luke 24:27), or sometimes into a threefold categorization of "the Law, Prophets, and the Writings" (see a possible allusion to this in Luke 24:44, where "Psalms" is shorthand for "the Writings"). The Jewish Bible is still categorized according to law, prophets, and writings, while our Protestant Bible organizes the books more according to literary types: law, history, poetry, and prophecy (first Major Prophets, then Minor Prophets).[1]

Before describing particular books in the Old Testament, let's flesh out the threefold division (law, prophets, and writings) a little more. The first five books of the Bible, often referred to as the "law of Moses," are also referred to as the "Torah" or the "Pentateuch." "Torah" is a Hebrew word that means "instruction" or "law." So when it's used to refer to the first five books of the Bible, it emphasizes these books as God's law. The term "Pentateuch" (from Greek, *pentateukos*) starts with "*penta*" (Greek for "five") and highlights these books as a five-volume compilation: Genesis through Deuteronomy. After the law of Moses comes the prophets. These included many of the books from Joshua to Ezekiel, as well as the collection of twelve books commonly called the "Minor Prophets." The third and last division ("the Writings") included Psalms, Proverbs, Job,

Song of Solomon, Ruth, Lamentations, Ecclesiastes, Esther, Daniel, Ezra, Nehemiah, and 1 and 2 Chronicles.

"THE WRITINGS"	PSALMS	PROVERBS	JOB	SOLOMON'S SONG	RUTH	LAMENTATIONS	ECCLESIASTES	ESTHER	DANIEL	EZRA	NEHEMIAH	1 CHRONICLES	2 CHRONICLES
"THE PROPHETS"	JOSHUA	JUDGES	1 SAMUEL	2 SAMUEL	1 KINGS	2 KINGS	ISAIAH	JEREMIAH	EZEKIEL	THE TWELVE MINOR PROPHETS			
"THE LAW"	GENESIS		EXODUS		LEVITICUS		NUMBERS		DEUTERONOMY				

Now, let's take a deeper dive into the content of the Old Testament books before moving on to the concept of "covenant," which is one of the central concepts in understanding the Old Testament.

THE CONTENT OF THE LAW

IT CAN BE A little confusing to set out to read the five books of the law and realize that, instead of lists of laws, it starts with stories. In fact, much of the content of the first five books of the Bible is narrative. Although these books do include the content of the laws God provided Israel, they are set in the unfolding of history as God shaped his chosen people. These first five books provide ancient Israel with a historical perspective of their development into a people beginning with the first man, Adam, and culminating with their preparation to receive the promised land of Canaan.

The order of the first five books—Genesis, Exodus, Leviticus, Numbers, and Deuteronomy—follows a chronological order of historical events. After narrating God's creation of the world, Genesis describes the apostasy of mankind (Genesis 3–11) and then the formation of a chosen people through Abraham (Genesis 12–50). Genesis gives ancient Israel a documented history of their founding in the twelve sons of Abraham's grandson Jacob/Israel (the "twelve tribes of Israel") and their subsequent move to Egypt to survive (through God's providentially working through Joseph) during the famine (Genesis 50:19–20). This ultimately sets up the reader to prepare to understand their dramatic exodus from Egypt (narrated in the book of Exodus).

After the Jewish people in Egypt were enslaved, God brought them out of Egyptian bondage through Moses (Exodus 3:7–11). The reader is invited into the experience of how God moved Israel from being slaves in a foreign nation to becoming his covenant people. After God delivered them from Egypt through a series of miracles, they received God's law at Mount Sinai (Exodus 19–24).

We read many more of God's laws in the book of Leviticus as well as in the book of Numbers. Leviticus is named after the Israelite tribe of Levi, which was set apart to serve in the temple; hence, Leviticus contains laws detailing such rituals as temple sacrifices. Numbers narrates how the Israelites were numbered according to tribe in order to prepare for their entrance into the promised land.

The people of God had lost their resolve to enter the promised land, so they wandered, even as God led them, in the wilderness. They wandered for decades before they were ready to finally enter the land. At the culmination of this wandering, Moses prepared Israel to take possession of the promised land prior to his death. Before entering, the new generation was reminded of God's law, which was told to them in the book of Deuteronomy (a word meaning "second law").

From a theological perspective, these first five books begin to unfold God's purpose to destroy the works of the serpent, who tempted the first humans to reject God's authority (Genesis 3). God created a good world that was cursed when Adam and Eve chose to obey the serpent's words over God's. In Genesis 3:15, God declared his purpose to eventually defeat evil through the "woman's offspring." This prophecy is commonly referred to as the "proto-evangelium" (Greek for "first gospel") in which God declared that the offspring of the woman would be victorious over the offspring of the serpent, resulting in the crushing of the serpent's head. This enmity between the people of God and the forces of evil was displayed throughout Old Testament history, beginning with the conflict of Cain and Abel (Genesis 4:1–8) and continuing on through the church's perpetual conflict with Satan as they follow Jesus in the face of persecution.

This promise of victory over the serpent was ultimately achieved by Jesus:

> The one who does what is sinful is of the devil, because the devil has been sinning from the beginning. The reason the Son of God appeared was to destroy the devil's work. (1 John 3:8)

Similarly, Paul declares victory for the church over Satan during the days of antagonism from the Roman Empire:

> Everyone has heard about your obedience, so I rejoice because of you; but I want you to be wise about what is good, and innocent about what is evil. The God of peace will soon crush Satan under your feet. The grace of our Lord Jesus be with you. (Romans 16:19– 20)

To this end, clearly the events of the Pentateuch should be understood through its own announcement of the promise of God to destroy the works of the serpent, later revealed to be Satan himself (Revelation 20:2). Every subsequent move of the hand of God in the history of humanity, Israel, and the church is to fulfill this promise.

THE CONTENT OF THE PROPHETS

THE PROPHETS IS THE second division of the Hebrew Old Testament. These books often include what's categorized as the Former Prophets, the Later Prophets, and the Minor Prophets (the Minor Prophets is also known as the Book of the Twelve).

- The Former Prophets: Joshua, Judges, Samuel, Kings
- The Later Prophets: Isaiah, Jeremiah, Ezekiel
- The Minor Prophets (the Twelve): Hosea, Joel, Amos, Obadiah, Jonah, Micah, Nahum, Habakkuk, Zephaniah, Haggai, Zechariah, Malachi

The writings of the Former Prophets are actually part of what are known in the Protestant Bible as the books of history. These books describe Israel's conquest and settlement in the land of Canaan, where they were ruled, first by Israelite judges and then by Israelite kings. The book of Joshua is named after Moses's successor who led them into Canaan. The book of Judges describes a pattern of Israel's rebellion against God, followed by God's deliverance from foreign nations through raising up Israelite judges. The books of Samuel and the Kings cover Israel's ups and downs under the reign of a kingship system beginning with King Saul, eventually splitting into two kingdoms ("Israel" in the north, "Judah" in the south), which were both defeated and carried into exile by foreign empires (the north by Assyria, the south by Babylon).

The Later Prophets include three of the prophets known in the Protestant Bible as Major Prophets: Isaiah, Jeremiah, Ezekiel. The Minor Prophets are shorter books also known as the "Twelve" (e.g., in the Greek Bible known as the Septuagint). It is noteworthy that these Minor Prophets are called "minor" only on the basis of their length and not based on their significance. It is plausible that Stephen, the first Christian martyr, references these books in Acts 7:42 in his speech to the Jewish authorities when he mentions the "book of the prophets" and goes on to reference Amos 5:25–27.

These prophetic books continued to lead Israel through the dissolution of its kingdoms—the northern and southern tribes—and throughout their captivity among foreign nations. Prophets reminded the people to follow God's laws and not to lose hope of future restoration, even through very difficult times. For example, Israel and Judah's experiences at the hands of Assyria shed light on the books of Hosea, Amos, and Micah. The demise of Assyria and the rise of Babylon function as the background for Nahum, Habakkuk, and Zephaniah. The restoration of Judah under the Persian Empire provides context to the books of Haggai, Zechariah, and Malachi.

PROPHETS REMINDED THE PEOPLE TO FOLLOW GOD'S LAWS.

THE CONTENT OF THE WRITINGS

THE WRITINGS CONSIST OF:

- The Psalms: a book of 150 songs to be used in worship
- The Proverbs: a collection of wise sayings for ethical instruction
- Job: a book of poetry following the tragedies of a follower of God trying to determine the source of his sufferings
- The Song of Songs: a poetic celebration of romantic love
- Ruth: a story of a Moabite woman who accepts the Jewish God and joins the Jewish people
- Lamentations: reflections on the fall of Jerusalem to the Babylonians

- Ecclesiastes: reflections on the meaning of life in an often-senseless world
- Esther: the story of a Jewish woman who becomes a Persian queen
- Daniel: a book that records both history and prophecy through the lens of a trusted Jewish official in Babylon during the exile
- Ezra–Nehemiah: a narration of the rebuilding of the Jewish homeland after their return under the Persians
- Chronicles: a record of the events of Samuel and Kings

The Writings were used to explicate life under the law, facilitate worship, and function as a corpus of wisdom literature. Five of these—the Song of Songs, Ruth, Lamentations, Ecclesiastes, and Esther—form a category known as "the Five" or *Megilloth*, meant to be publicly read, one at each of the five major Jewish holidays.

The Hebrew Bible makes a total of twenty-four books. Why then does the Protestant Bible list thirty-nine books? It's the same content packaged differently. The books of Samuel, Kings, and Chronicles are each divided into two parts (e.g., 1 and 2 Samuel). Ezra–Nehemiah is treated as two books. The Minor Prophets are listed as twelve separate books.

As mentioned earlier, it is also common for the Protestant Bible to use a different categorization than the Hebrew Bible, so the books are listed in the basic progression of law (Genesis–Deuteronomy); history (Joshua–Esther); poetry (Job–Song of Solomon, sometimes referred to as wisdom literature); and prophecy (both Major and Minor Prophets).

LAW	Genesis, Exodus, Leviticus, Numbers, Deuteronomy
HISTORY	Joshua, Judges, Ruth, 1 Samuel, 2 Samuel, 1 Kings, 2 Kings, 1 Chronicles, 2 Chronicles, Ezra, Nehemiah, Esther
POETRY	Job, Psalms, Proverbs, Ecclesiastes, Song of Songs
MAJOR PROPHETS	Isaiah, Jeremiah, Lamentations, Ezekiel, Daniel
MINOR PROPHETS	Hosea, Joel, Amos, Obadiah, Jonah, Micah, Nahum, Habakkuk, Zephaniah, Haggai, Zechariah, Malachi

UNDERSTANDING THE OLD TESTAMENT AS COVENANT

As I mentioned, "Old Testament" can carry one of two different meanings. Let's focus now on the second, less common meaning, which refers to the old covenant law given by God through Moses. When biblical writers of both the Old and New Testaments speak of a "new covenant," this implies the existence of an old covenant. The author of the New Testament book of Hebrews contrasts the two covenants and draws the conclusion that the new covenant is superior, built on better promises and through an even better lawgiver than Moses. Such an argument was designed to dissuade the Jewish recipients of the letter from retreating back into Judaism. Hebrews 8:6 explains that Jesus "has obtained a more excellent ministry, to the extent that He is also the mediator of a better covenant, which has been enacted on better promises" (NASB). The writer of Hebrews goes on to contrast this covenant through Jesus with the "first covenant," which was broken by the people. With the first covenant broken, God sought to establish a "second" covenant, which was predicted by the Old Testament prophet Jeremiah (Jeremiah 31:31–34).

This old covenant was the law given to Israel at Mount Sinai, summarized in the Ten Commandments. Taken altogether, the law functioned as a national law to govern the people of God. Through their acceptance of the covenant stipulations, God would make Israel a people for his own possession, a holy nation, and a kingdom of priests (Exodus 19:5–6). This covenant would inaugurate the formal relationship between God and his chosen people. The content of the law would explain their relationship to the God who delivered them from bondage, and their interpersonal relationship with the community of Israel. It was Jesus who explained the vertical (between God and people) and horizontal nature (person to person) of God's covenant laws in Matthew 22:34–40:

> Hearing that Jesus had silenced the Sadducees, the Pharisees got together. One of them, an expert in the law, tested him with this question: "Teacher, which is the greatest commandment in the Law?" Jesus replied: "'Love the Lord your God with all your heart and with all your soul and with all your mind.' This is the first and greatest commandment. And the second is like it: 'Love your neighbor as yourself.' All the Law and the Prophets hang on these two commandments." (Matthew 22:34–40)

To accent that the law teaches relationship to God and people, Jesus quoted the two greatest commandments, originally given in Deuteronomy 6:4–5 and Leviticus 19:18. In essence, the law taught to love God and love people. This covenant law anticipated the coming of the Messiah and exposed the people's need for this person.

The anticipation of his coming is expressed in Galatians 3:24–5. Paul refers to the law as a guardian that leads to Jesus: "Therefore the Law has become our guardian to lead us to Christ, so that we may be justified by faith. But now that faith has come, we are no longer under a guardian" (Galatians 3:24–25, NASB). The context here is Paul's effort to correct the folly of trying to use our obedience to the old covenant law as our grounds of our righteousness. Instead, he argues

THE LAW TAUGHT TO LOVE GOD AND LOVE PEOPLE.

the purpose of the law was to lead to the "Messiah" (a Hebrew word translated into Greek to sound like our English word *Christ*). Additionally, the law served as a legal system condemning the law breaker at the first infraction. In other words, to be guilty of breaking one law makes one guilty of the entire system.

And if the law's elaborate system of animal sacrifices teaches us anything, it is that God does not leave guilt unpunished. Paul states it this way:

> For all who rely on the works of the law are under a curse, as it is written: "Cursed is everyone who does not continue to do everything written in the Book of the Law." Clearly no one who relies on the law is justified before God, because "the righteous will live by faith." The law is not based on faith; on the contrary, it says, "The person who does these things will live by them." (Galatians 3:10–12)

Do any of us obey "everything written in the Book of the Law"? According to Paul, one who does not practice maintaining the entire law remains under condemnation. That's not good news, but it sets us up to be ready to hear the *good news*—a phrase encapsulated in the New Testament word "gospel." So we see the Old Testament—as thirty-nine books of Israelite history, prophecy, *and* as a system of laws—cultivates a longing for the Messiah to come and make things right. The Old Testament narrates a broken covenant and promises a new one.

It is to this Messiah, Jesus, and his new covenant that we now turn.

REFLECTION & DISCUSSION QUESTIONS

1. Why is it important to understand the layout of the Bible in general? Why the Old Testament in particular?

_____

_____

_____

_____

_____

2. Why might God have chosen to give us his truth in an unfolding set of historical events?

_____

_____

_____

_____

_____

3. What is the significance of God's promise in
   Genesis 3:15 for understanding salvation?

_____

_____

_____

_____

_____

_____

4. Recall the three main categories of books in the
   Old Testament? Which books go in each category?

_____

_____

_____

_____

_____

_____

5. What are some of the key differences between the old covenant and the new covenant laid out in this chapter?

_____

_____

_____

_____

_____

_____

6. Why was it necessary for God to make a "second" covenant?

_____

_____

_____

_____

_____

_____

_____

2

WHAT IS THE NEW TESTAMENT?

Answer: The New Testament is the apostles' teachings in twenty-seven books that reveal a new covenant through Jesus the Messiah and how the covenant was lived out in the early church.

This is the covenant I will make with the people of Israel after that time," declares the LORD. "I will put my law in their minds and write it on their hearts. I will be their God, and they will be my people.
— Jeremiah 31:33

The Old Testament ends without a resolution. Although God had been faithful to bring his people back from exile to return and rebuild their homeland, the vast majority of Old Testament prophecies remained unfulfilled at the end of the Hebrew Bible. The final words of the final prophet (Malachi) promised the reappearance of Elijah, who would turn the "hearts of the children to their fathers." And if they rejected the Godsent message, God would "strike the land with complete destruction" (Malachi 4:5–6, NASB). Who was this "Elijah" who was going to come again? In a parallel prediction, Malachi had also promised, "Behold, I am sending My messenger, and he will clear a way before Me. And the Lord, whom you are seeking, will suddenly come to His temple" (Malachi 3:1, NASB).

Although the events of the New Testament take place some four hundred years after the Old Testament's final book, the New Testament begins where the Old Testament leaves off. For starters, John the Baptist served as the Elijah "to come." His birth to aged, previously infertile parents was followed soon by the birth of Jesus, the Messiah, to a virgin betrothed to be married. John the Baptist grew up and became the "voice of one calling in the wilderness, 'Prepare the way for the Lord'" (Matthew 3:3). John pointed his followers to Jesus as Messiah, and in turn Jesus confirmed that "John himself is Elijah who was to come" (Matthew 11:14,

NASB). In step with Malachi's prediction, Jesus came to Jerusalem's temple, preached the gospel to a people who predominantly rejected him (John 1:11), and predicted destruction for the city and sacred site (Matthew 24:2; Luke 23:28–31). The rest is history from there.

OVERVIEW OF THE NEW TESTAMENT CONTENT

THE NEW TESTAMENT NARRATES the life, ministry, death, and resurrection of Jesus as well as the establishment of his kingdom. His kingdom expanded throughout the then-known world, beginning with the Jews and extending to the non-Jewish world (the Gentiles). Like the Old Testament, these books cover a variety of genres such as historical narratives, letters, and apocalyptic literature. The four Gospels—Matthew, Mark, Luke, and John—are historical narratives that describe the ministry of Jesus, which culminates with his resurrection and commission of his disciples to make disciples all over the world. The New Testament also includes a history of the early church called the book of Acts.

Additionally, we have letters (also known as "epistles") written to churches and individuals, which provide instructions with regard to faith and practice. These letters can be categorized into Pauline Letters (written by Paul to specific churches and individuals) and General Letters (written by various authors without a clearly designated audience in view). The General Letters, also called "Catholic Letters" ("catholic" simply means "universal"), include correspondences written by James, Peter, John, and Jude, as well as the anonymous letter of Hebrews. The Bible ends with a prophetic book called Revelation. Most present-day Bibles—whether Protestant, Catholic, or Eastern Orthodox—arrange the books of the New Testament according to the following basic order:[2]

GOSPELS	HISTORY	LETTERS OF PAUL	GENERAL LETTERS	APOCALYPSE
Matthew	Acts of the Apostles	Romans	Hebrews	Revelation
Mark		1 Corinthians	James	
Luke		2 Corinthians	1 Peter	
John		Galatians	2 Peter	
		Ephesians	1 John	
		Philippians	2 John	
		Colossians	3 John	
		1 Thessalonians	Jude	
		2 Thessalonians		
		1 Timothy		
		2 Timothy		
		Titus		
		Philemon		

THE CONTENT OF THE GOSPELS

The Greek word translated "gospel" (*euangelion*) originally meant "good news." The word became an appropriate word for the long-awaited message Jesus came to bring because he came with a message of hope for the hopeless and freedom for the oppressed. The Gospels were ancient biographies written to teach us about the life and ministry of Jesus.[3] For example, the first words of Jesus recorded in the Gospel of Mark are: "The time is fulfilled, and the kingdom of God is at hand; repent and believe in the gospel" (Mark 1:15, NASB). Then, when four narrations of the life of Jesus were written by his apostles or by close friends of the apostles, it also made sense to call these four documents "Gospels."

The four Gospels taught the life of Jesus from four vantage points to four unique audiences. Because of their similar narrative order, as well as some shared content, Matthew, Mark, and Luke are considered the "Synoptic Gospels" ("synoptic" meaning "to see together"). John's Gospel is not considered a Synoptic Gospel because of its significant number of unparalleled information from the other three Gospels. Even so, each Gospel has its own unique fingerprint.

Matthew. The Gospel According to Matthew was written with a Jewish audience in mind. This is evident because Matthew's Gospel quotes a good deal of Old

Testament passages with the intent of showing their fulfillment with the coming of Jesus as the predicted Messiah. A significant word found throughout the fabric of Matthew is "fulfill" or "fulfilled." After narrating an event in Jesus' life, Matthew often connects it to the Old Testament: for example, "This took place to fulfill what the Lord had said through the prophet" (Matthew 1:22), and, "This has all taken place that the writings of the prophets might be fulfilled" (Matthew 26:56). "Fulfill" or "fulfilled" is used sixteen times in the book of Matthew, and the majority of the references draw a connection between Jesus and an Old Testament foreshadowing.

Additionally, the theme of the "kingdom of heaven" runs throughout the Gospel of Matthew. In the days of Jesus, there was a clear expectation of the coming of the kingdom of God, which had been predicted by the Old Testament writers. Many of the Jewish people of Jesus' day had anticipated a militaristic kingdom, but there was often a mismatch between expectations and Jesus' message. Yet through his many parables in the Gospel of Matthew, Jesus painted an inviting, even if surprising, picture of a kingdom that would conquer far more than a physical army could ever do. This kingdom of righteousness—described so comprehensively in Matthew's Sermon on the Mount—was a limitless treasure (Matthew 13:44) that would outlast the powers of darkness. In it, "the righteous will shine like the sun in the kingdom of their Father" (Matthew 13:43).

Mark. The Gospel According to Mark was written to a predominantly Gentile audience. We see this in how Mark describes Jewish customs (Mark 7:1–5) and phrases (Mark 5:41; 7:34; 10:46; 15:22, 34) as though his audience was unfamiliar with these things. The Gospel of Mark invites the Christian to embrace humble service as exemplified in Jesus Christ, as he explains: "Whoever wants to become great among you must be your servant. . . . For even the Son of Man did not come to be served, but to serve, and to give his life as a ransom for many" (Mark 10:43, 45). Mark's Gospel also concerns itself with the coming of the kingdom of God. Mark uses the phrase the "kingdom of God" in parallel with the "kingdom of heaven" language in the Gospel of Matthew. Then, whereas Matthew's Gospel intersperses Jesus' miraculous deeds with sermons, Mark's Gospel tends to focus more on Jesus' miracles in a fast-paced narrative that spends the final third of the book on Jesus' final week in Jerusalem before his resurrection.

Luke. The Gospel According to Luke was written to the "most excellent Theophilus" (Luke 1:3). His title suggested he was a Roman official. This Gospel was an investigated account, in which Luke carefully and accurately researched the testimony of witnesses. Through a meticulous process of documenting historical detail,

Luke provides a detailed sketch of the life, death, and resurrection of Christ. His stated purpose was that Theophilus would know the "certainty" of the gospel (Luke 1:4)

The Gospel of Luke uniquely emphasizes Jesus' mission to *all* of humanity, from hopeless sinners to historic outcasts. This is not surprising, given that Luke seems to be the only Gentile author in the New Testament (with the possible exception of Hebrews). Jesus' intention to reach outside of conventional molds for making disciples can be seen in some of the parables unique to Luke's Gospel, such as the parable of the prodigal son, the parable of the good Samaritan, and the parable of the pharisee and the tax collector. Luke, a close friend of the apostle Paul, wrote his Gospel as the first in a two-part series ending with the book of Acts.

John. The Gospel According to John is considered the last of the four Gospels to be written. Written by Jesus' disciple John in his old age, this document combines a simple style with theological reflections on the events that happened when John was a young man. While the Synoptic Gospels displayed Jesus' divine nature, for example, in instances such as being incarnated and born of a virgin (Luke 1:35), forgiving sins (Matthew 9:4–6), receiving worship (Matthew 14:33), and calling himself divine names (Matthew 27:43)—the Gospel of John makes Jesus' divinity a point of emphasis.

John's opening prologue places an accent on the theological truth that God became flesh: "In the beginning was the Word, and the Word was with God, and the Word was God," and, "The Word became flesh and made his dwelling among us" (John 1:1, 14). The author strategically chooses a set of seven miracles as manifestations of Jesus' divine glory. The author explains that many signs were done among the disciples, yet the ones written were so the reader would believe that Jesus is the Son of God (John 20:31–31).

The Gospel of John also includes seven "I am" statements in which Jesus fleshes out his character in a manner that matches God's way of referring to himself. In Exodus 3:14, God told Moses, "I AM WHO I AM," when Moses asked his name. In the same way, Jesus uses language that accents his divinity so the reader can clearly see the uniqueness of his sonship. For example, "I am the bread of life" (John 6:35), "I am the light of the world" (John 8:12), and "I am the way and the truth and the life" (John 14:6). At one point, Jesus even told a shocked audience, "Before Abraham was born, I am!" (John 8:58). This Gospel was written during the rise of what became known as "Gnostic" teachings, which rejected the importance of physical substance; thus, John wrote in part to remind people of the truth that God indeed came in the flesh.

The Gospels provide a comprehensive portrait of Jesus, allowing the readers to see his central place in the scheme of redemption. The climactic death, burial, and resurrection is the destination of each Gospel while narrating different snapshots of his life and teachings to arrive at this target.

THE HISTORY OF THE CHURCH IN ACTS

THE BOOK OF ACTS plays a crucial part in the New Testament. As mentioned above, Acts is the second part of Luke's two-volume work meant to show the recipient, Theophilus, the truthfulness of Christianity. In this second volume, Luke highlights the spread of the gospel under the guidance of the Holy Spirit, who had been given to all who believed (Acts 2:17–21). Acts 1:8 is a central passage that provides a geographical outline of the book of Acts: Jesus promised, "You will receive power when the Holy Spirit has come upon you; and you shall be My witnesses both in Jerusalem and in all Judea, and Samaria, and as far as the remotest part of the earth" (NASB). Jesus' disciples went from Jerusalem (Acts 1–2) to Judea and Samaria (Acts 3–8), and the "remotest part of the

THE GOSPELS PROVIDE A COMPREHENSIVE PORTRAIT OF JESUS.

earth" was a figurative way of expressing "Gentile territory" (Acts 9–28).

In Jerusalem during a celebration of the Jewish festival of Pentecost, the Holy Spirit came upon the apostles. As a result, they began to speak supernaturally in the native languages of the gathered celebrants. On that first day, three thousand people were baptized into Jesus, and the church began devoting themselves to "the apostles' teaching and to fellowship, to the breaking of bread and to prayer" (Acts 2:42).

As I mentioned, Acts explains how the gospel spread outward from Jerusalem, reaching people as diverse from each other as an Ethiopian government official (Acts 8), a Roman centurion (Acts 10), a Greek jailer (Acts 16), and—very notably—a Jewish Pharisee who had hated the new faith and tried to stamp it out by force (Acts 9). While the apostle Peter took a central role in the first chapters of the book, it was the former hater of the faith—Luke's mentor Paul—whose missionary travels take center stage for the latter half of the book. Acts ends with Paul's arrival as a prisoner at the seat of imperial power: Rome. Acts describes a church that faced persecution with resilience and theological disputes with grace, truth, and dependence on the Holy Spirit.

PAULINE LETTERS

PAUL WAS RESPONSIBLE FOR writing thirteen letters of the New Testament. Having accomplished three recorded missionary journeys, Paul had a tremendous influence over the churches throughout the known world at the time. These letters cover a variety of circumstances. Several of the letters express Paul's intimate relationship with the churches he planted. The different occasions birth a variety of thematic emphases.

Throughout the letters of Paul, we find efforts to bring clarity to the doctrine of the grace of God, explaining that the law was not a means to establishing right standing with God. While the law of Moses exposed sin, it was incapable of eradicating sin. This thematic emphasis is seen in letters such as Romans and Galatians. The heresy of binding the Jewish law upon Gentiles as a means for them to obtain righteousness before God was designated by Paul as a "different gospel" (Galatians 1:6–10).

In other letters like the Corinthians correspondences, Paul takes on a pastoral posture when troubleshooting malignant behaviors within the life of the congregation. We can see this in 1 and 2 Corinthians when Paul addressed a spirit of division that permeated the church at Corinth. Their divisions arose from a number of issues. For example, some of them separated into factions based on which preacher had delivered the gospel to them (1 Corinthians 1:10–13). They took each other before the law for trivial matters (1 Corinthians 6). They engaged in practices such as eating meat offered to idols, which was insensitive toward fellow Christians (1 Corinthians 8). They manifested arrogance over whose gift was superior in the church (1 Corinthians 12).

It is also common to witness Paul as an encourager promoting unity and faithfulness among believers. Take, for example, his letter to a Christian named Philemon to appeal that Philemon accept back his escaped slave, "no longer as a slave, but better than a slave, as a dear brother" (Philemon 1:16), or his letter to the Philippians, inviting a disposition of joy in the midst of their suffering as a church. There are letters with end times concerns, in which the letter is intended to clarify the nature of our hope in Christ. There are also the "Pastoral Epistles"—1 and 2 Timothy and Titus—by which Paul sought to explain "how people ought to conduct themselves in God's household, which is the church of the living God, the pillar and foundation of the truth" (1 Timothy 3:15). The Pauline epistles account for almost half of the New Testament and provide insight into the ethics of the church and early Christian worship (e.g., Christ-centered "hymns" recorded in Philippians 2:5–11 and Colossians 1:15–20).

GENERAL EPISTLES

THE GENERAL EPISTLES WERE written to more generic audiences of Christians, and not limited to Christians in one geographical location. They were wider in scope. These letters include James, 1 and 2 Peter, 1, 2, and 3 John, and Jude (and sometimes Hebrews). The letter of James was written by James—the half-brother to Jesus and early leader in the Jerusalem church. It focuses on practical living, and James articulates how the gospel can be lived out in everyday scenarios and how trials produce patience.

The letters of the apostle Peter (1 and 2 Peter) were written in a hostile climate under the rule of Emperor Nero and encouraged Christians to remain faithful as they endured suffering. Both James and Peter were eventually martyred, James in Jerusalem and Peter in Rome.[4] The apostle John, also considered to be the author of the Gospel and Revelation, wrote the letters of 1, 2, and 3 John to encourage orthodoxy in the face of the Gnostic-like teaching that I mentioned. Like James, Jude was also a son of both Joseph and Mary, and he wrote the letter of Jude, charging his audience to "contend for the faith that was once for all entrusted to God's holy people" (Jude 1:3).

An argument can be made that the book of Hebrews is a general epistle, although it does not as naturally fit into this category. It is arranged more like a sermon than a letter. The anonymous author writes to a Jewish-Christian audience who was tempted to reject Jesus and revert back into Judaism. The content is a comprehensive argument that Jesus is superior to whatever elements of Judaism—angels, Moses, Joshua, etc.—might attract the recipient back into Judaism.

REVELATION

Revelation is a prophetic book written by the apostle John in the ancient genre of apocalypse. "Apocalypse" means "uncovering" or "revealing," and in the context of genre suggests the usage of rich literary symbolism. Thus, this book is appropriately called "Revelation" in English as it reveals King Jesus as being ultimately victorious in the cosmic war between good and evil. Numerous interpretive lenses offer themselves for reading Revelation, many of which are based on how to read the "thousand years" (a millennium) of Jesus' reign described in Revelation 20. Hence, the frameworks for understanding Revelation as a whole, which come from one's view of the millennium in Revelation 20, often have the word "millennium" in them (e.g., premillennialism, postmillennialism, amillennialism).

Regardless of one's interpretive framework, we can make clear observations about the book of Revelation:

The original recipients of this letter were Christians in Asia Minor (modern-day Turkey), who were facing persecution for the faith. John directly addressed the churches in seven cities of Asia Minor with a message from Jesus written specifically to each church at the beginning of the book (Revelation 2–3). Another useful observation is that within the twenty-two chapters comprising the book, there are around five hundred allusions to events and other features of the Old Testament. So anyone who wants to be a serious student of Revelation needs to be a serious student of the Old Testament as well. Finally, Revelation reveals how God meets frightening persecutions from anti-Christian governments with decisive judgments, all culminating in the return of King Jesus to judge evil once and for all. In the end, God will restore creation to the Eden-like relationship that existed between God and humans in the beginning.[5]

A SERIOUS STUDENT OF REVELATION NEEDS TO BE A SERIOUS STUDENT OF THE OLD TESTAMENT.

THE NEW TESTAMENT AS GOD'S NEW COVENANT LAW

As with the Old Testament, the New Testament is the name of a collection of documents (or "books"), but the term itself suggests a sacred promise between God and humans. The Greek word *diathēœkēœ* is a legal term that can mean "last will and testament" or "covenant" or "contract." The word is used approximately thirty-three times in the New Testament, and a significant number of those times refers to the new covenant law ratified by the blood of Christ that provides us with the promise of salvation from our sins.

The first usage of the term is found during Jesus' observance of Passover the evening before being crucified. Pulling from the imagery of the slain lamb during the Exodus (Exodus 12:7), whose blood covered the houses of the Hebrews at the time death entered Egypt, Jesus announced his blood would be the basis of our forgiveness: "This is my blood of the covenant, which is poured out for many for the forgiveness of sins" (Matthew 26:28).

When the New Testament speaks of the "blood of the covenant," it suggests that death was necessary to enforce the covenant. This was true of the old covenant (for example, the animals that were sacrificed), and also true of the new covenant. This is well expressed in Hebrews 9:15–17, where the Hebrew writer speaks of the necessity of the death of the one who makes the covenant, in the manner of a last will and testament. The passage says:

> For a covenant is valid only when people are dead, for it is never in force while the one who made it lives. Therefore even the first covenant was not inaugurated without blood. (Hebrews 9:17–18, NASB)

A key passage in understanding the new covenant is the predictive prophecy of Jeremiah where he contrasts the old covenant and new covenant.

> "For this is the covenant which I will make with the house of Israel after those days," declares the Lord: "I will put My law within them and write it on their heart; and I will be their God, and they shall be My people. They will not teach again, each one his neighbor and each one his brother, saying, 'Know the Lord,' for they will all know Me, from the least of them to the greatest of them," declares the Lord, "for I will forgive their wrongdoing, and their sin I will no longer remember." (Jeremiah 31:33–34, NASB)

God announced through Jeremiah that he would establish a new covenant that would stand in contrast to the old. The contrast is then specified as placing his laws within their hearts and not on tablets of stone as with the old covenant (2 Corinthians 3:2–3). The righteousness of God would emanate from an inward change and not simply an outward conforming to law. He would be their God, and they would be his people in an eternal relationship of knowing and being known.

The New Testament, therefore, is a covenant provided by God that offers forgiveness of sins and results in eternal salvation. This covenant is made known to us through the books of the New Testament that unfold God's scheme of redemption and the Christian faith. Understanding the content and the designations of the Old and New Testament provokes the question: *How did we get the Bible?*

REFLECTION & DISCUSSION QUESTIONS

1. What is something about each of the four Gospels that makes them unique?

   _____

   _____

   _____

   _____

   _____

2. Starting with the miraculous birth and ending with the resurrection, what are some of the major events of Jesus' life as told in the Gospels?

   _____

   _____

   _____

   _____

   _____

   _____

3. Why is the book of Acts important for disciples of Jesus to understand?

_____

_____

_____

_____

_____

_____

4. What are some of the doctrines taught in the letters of the New Testament (the "epistles")? Why are some of them called "General Epistles"?

_____

_____

_____

_____

_____

_____

_____

5. How can the Pauline letters be used to clarify, encourage, or promote unity in the church today?

_____

_____

_____

_____

_____

_____

6. In your own words, describe what is meant by the phrase "blood of the covenant." What is its significance in your life?

_____

_____

_____

_____

_____

_____

_____

3

HOW DID WE GET OUR BIBLE?

Answer: Our Bible has come together through a process guided through by God through his Holy Spirit, which includes revelation, inspiration, and canonization.

For prophecy never had its origin in the human will, but prophets, though human, spoke from God as they were carried along by the Holy Spirit.
— 2 Peter 1:21

The question of how we got our Bible requires a multifaceted answer. When the question is posed, some might refer to how we got the sixty-six books that are within our current Bible. Others might be asking about the process of how we went from God speaking to his people through spokespersons to having documented Scripture that is considered God's Word. Some might be curious how we got our current versions the Bible into our own languages and preferred styles. While each one of these questions makes for great discussions, this chapter will handle only the general process of how the Bible went from being God's spoken word to the written Word we call Scripture, which we believe to be the Word of God.

We must take important steps to trace rightly the journey from God's spoken word to the written Scriptures. The three key words we will spend the most time unpacking are *revelation*, *inspiration*, and *canonization*:

- Revelation means the process of God disclosing his will.
- Inspiration means God is the source of Scripture, safeguarding the transmission of his message.
- Canonization means the process by which the church recognized which writings would be included in Scripture.

Let's go through these one by one.

REVELATION

THE APOSTLE PAUL PENNED the book of Ephesians, likely writing to a predominantly Gentile audience. His intent was to display the plan of salvation as it accomplishes the bringing together of Jews and Gentiles into one spiritual body. Paul's usage of the word "revelation" in the context of the letter as a whole aids us in understanding how we got the Bible:

> For this reason I, Paul, the prisoner of Christ Jesus for the sake of you Gentiles—if indeed you have heard of the administration of God's grace which was given to me for you; *that by revelation* there was made known to me the mystery, *as I wrote* before briefly. By referring to this, *when you read you can understand* my insight into the mystery of Christ. (Ephesians 3:1–4, NASB)

A careful examination of this passage will provide a helpful way of understanding how we got the Bible. As Paul describes the plan of salvation, which began with God before time started, he refers to it as a "mystery" (Ephesians 3:3–6). The word "mystery" as used by Paul describes something kept secret until made known. This mystery, according to Ephesians 3:6, was the inclusion of the Gentiles alongside Jews in the body of Christ.

How was this mystery made known? The answer is given in verse three: "by revelation." "Revelation" here means to unfold, disclose, or to make known. Revelation is the unveiling of the will of God to the mind of a human vessel, so that a person has the opportunity to understand. After this, Paul mentions the documentation of the revelation, saying, "As I wrote before briefly" (Ephesians 3:3, NASB). Paul received revelation from God, and then made it known through his writing.

Unlike a deist god, who creates the world and then leaves it behind, the God of the Bible is intent on revealing himself and his will to people. Romans 1:20 explains, "Since the creation of the world God's invisible qualities—his eternal power and divine nature—have been clearly seen." The psalmist sings, "The heavens declare the glory of God; the skies proclaim the work of his hands. Day after day they pour forth speech; night after night they reveal knowledge" (Psalm 19:1–2). In addition to revealing himself through creation, God revealed himself and his will throughout the Bible through such conduits as dreams (Numbers 12:6), laws (Deuteronomy 29:29), audible words (1 Samuel 3:21), predictions (2 Kings 8:10), visions (Daniel 2:19), and miracles (John 2:11). Through the Son, God revealed himself most fully (Hebrews 1:1–4). This desire to make himself known to people continues from the Bible's opening pages, where God called out after Adam sinned, "Where are you?" (Genesis 3:9) to its closing chapters in Revelation.

INSPIRATION

WHEN GOD'S REVELATION IS written down, it is then called inspired Scripture. It is the Word of God documented. As mentioned earlier, both the Old and the New Testaments are referred in the Bible as Scripture. Consider a common passage that we used in the introduction of this book.

> And that from childhood you have known
> the sacred writings which are able to give you
> the wisdom that leads to salvation through
> faith which is in Christ Jesus. All Scripture is
> inspired by God and beneficial for teaching,
> for rebuke, for correction, for training in
> righteousness; so that the man or woman of God
> may be fully capable, equipped for every good
> work. (2 Timothy 3:15–17, NASB)

This letter from Paul finds its occasion in the intent to encourage a timid Timothy for the work of ministry in the city of Ephesus. Paul indicates that Timothy was reared from childhood to know the Old Testament Scriptures, which were able to make him wise in regard to salvation. Paul goes on to describe the nature of

Scripture as being "inspired" or "God-breathed." This speaks to the divine origin of Scripture. God should be understood as the source of Scripture.

Additionally, inspiration involves the supervision of the Holy Spirit to move the human vessel to speak or document what God has revealed. God discloses himself and his will in various ways (i.e., revelation), and the Holy Spirit inspires the writer to write it down (inspiration). In 2 Peter 1:16–21, Peter speaks to this truth:

GOD'S REVELATION WRITTEN DOWN IS CALLED INSPIRED SCRIPTURE.

> But know this first of all, that no prophecy of Scripture becomes a matter of someone's own interpretation, for no prophecy was ever made by an act of human will, but men moved by the Holy Spirit spoke from God. (2 Peter 1:20–21, NASB)

A pivotal word in 2 Peter 1:21 in the context is the word "moved." This word is in the passive voice, which suggests that the human vessel is being acted upon. He is being guided by the Holy Spirit, who is the ultimate author of what is spoken. To this end, inspiration includes God safeguarding his message as it is spoken by human vessels led by the Holy Spirit.

This confidence in inspired Scripture is further undergirded in Acts 1:16, when the apostles were looking to choose someone to replace the traitorous disciple Judas. The same Peter announced the Scriptures must be fulfilled and a new apostle be chosen (Psalm 109:8). Notice what Peter's statement says about the origin and authoritativeness of Scripture:

> "Brothers, the Scripture had to be fulfilled, *which the Holy Spirit foretold by the mouth of David concerning Judas*, who became a guide to those who arrested Jesus. (Acts 1:16, NASB)

This passage implies David was not the original source of these words; rather, the Holy Spirit inspired David to speak these prophecies. Additionally, when David's spoken word became a written word, it was called "Scripture."

Over and over, we see the Old Testament writers believing themselves to be speaking words inspired by God, prefacing their statements by saying, "This is what the Lord says." Jesus shared this conviction, believing Scripture to be unbreakable (John 10:35) and forever (Matthew 5:17–18). Moreover, he believed the entirety of Old Testament Scripture pointed to him (Luke 24:25–27). In addition, Jesus promised the Holy Spirit would guide the apostles into all truth

(John 16:13–16), in which they would be moved by the Holy Spirit as were the Old Testament prophets. Accordingly, even as the New Testament was in the process of being written, we find its authors reference New Testament passages as Scripture (1 Timothy 5:17–18; 2 Peter 3:15–16).

If the Bible is God's inspired Word, as Jesus and the biblical writers taught, then the next logical step is to affirm its truthfulness, a conviction I develop further in Chapter 5.

CANONIZATION

"Canonization" refers to the process of recognizing which books were considered Scripture by the people of God at the time of compiling the Bible as we know it today. The term "canon" suggests a standard.[6] Ultimately, when discussing the idea of canon as it relates to the Bible, we are speaking about those books that are considered the standard of the Christian faith. At times, people have come to the erroneous conclusion that the books of the Bible were chosen by a select few people. However, canonization had more to do with recognition of the books that were already in circulation and accepted as authoritative within the context of God's covenant people.

The *Anchor Bible Dictionary* provides a synopsis of the term *canon* stating:

> The word "canon" comes from the Gk *kanōn*, "measuring stick." By extension it came to mean "rule" or "standard," a tool used for determining proper measurement. Consequently, the word has come to be used with reference to the corpus of scriptural writings that is considered authoritative and standard for defining and determining "orthodox" religious beliefs and practices.[7]

Jesus and his apostles assumed the canon of the Hebrew Old Testament. The New Testament either cites or alludes to the vast majority of Old Testament books, a fact which attests to the widespread acceptance of the Old Testament's canonicity and authority by Jesus, the New Testament authors, and the Jews in their time. In addition, the argument could be made that Jesus considers the entire spectrum of Old Testament canon when he mentions "the blood of righteous Abel to the blood of Zechariah" (Matthew 23:35). The mention of these two righteous men put to death by godless people spans the Old Testament from the Hebrew Bible's first book (Genesis) to its final book according to the Hebrew Bible listing (2 Chronicles).

The process of a canon of the New Testament was already set in place by the last words of Jesus to his apostles. In Matthew 28:18–20, Jesus told the apostles it was their duty to make other disciples using the teachings that he had given to them:

> Then Jesus came to them and said, "All authority in heaven and on earth has been given to me. Therefore go and make disciples of all nations, baptizing them in the name of the Father and of the Son and of the Holy Spirit, and teaching them to obey everything I have commanded you. And surely I am with you always, to the very end of the age."

The teachings of Jesus, given through the apostles, formed the basis of the canon or standard of objective truth. This is why the earliest church devoted themselves to the apostles' teachings in Acts 2:42: "They devoted themselves to the apostles' teaching and to fellowship, to the breaking of bread and to prayer." So the teachings and writings of the apostles—sometimes written down by their associates—formed the core of teachings of the new covenant. The existence of recognized books of the New Testament is found within the New Testament books themselves.

For instance, as mentioned earlier, Peter recognized Paul's writings as Scripture (2 Peter 3:15–16). Paul cites from Luke's Gospel (1 Timothy 5:17–18). Paul commanded that his letters be read to other churches (1 Thessalonians 5:27; Colossians 4:16). These are all clear indications that there were accepted letters that functioned as authoritative to the church.

The books in the New Testament were all written before the end of the first century (that is, before AD 100).[8] New Testament scholar Michael Kruger, an expert in the formation of the canon of the New Testament, describes the attitude of the church's leaders following the first century:

> Early Christians had a high view of the apostolic office, viewing the apostles as the very mouthpiece of Christ himself. Thus any document containing apostolic teaching would have been received as an authoritative written text (and the beginning of the canon).[9]

However, after the first century, these writings were not the only ones in circulation that claimed authoritativeness. In order to protect Christians from false teaching after the death of all the apostles, the early leaders needed to delineate writings that were apostolic—and therefore the authoritative words of Jesus—from those which were not. Some books claimed authority but were, in reality, written in later centuries by people falsely claiming to be Jesus' apostles (for example, the Gospel of Thomas and the Gospel of Peter). All the while, there was a core of first-century books that were recognized early on as being part of the canon (the four Gospels, Acts, Paul's epistles, etcetera), as well as early books that were not as quickly recognized by all regions of the church but came to be recognized as part of the canon (e.g., Hebrews and James). Kruger explains:

> Not only was there a "core" canon of the New Testament books that were well established from early time, but disagreements over peripheral canonical books were less problematic than is often portrayed.[10]

After persecution subsided and the church as a whole was able to publicly gather in the fourth century, they were able to land on an authoritative list of inspired books that comprised the New Testament. The early Christians recognized as authoritative those books that met three key criteria:[11]

1. The authoritative book had to be written by apostolic authors (or authors who were closely associated with apostles).
2. They taught the orthodox faith of the apostles.

3. They had been widely accepted in earliest churches from the beginning.

In order for the church at large to recognize what books had already long been accepted as authoritative by the churches, it measured the books by these standards. Recall the literal meaning of the word "canon" as "measuring stick." We see lists containing core New Testament books. For example, the Muratorian Fragment of the late second century includes the core books, even though, as only a fragment of the original document, the list is incomplete. Other lists include the full twenty-seven books as early as AD 250 (by Origen) and AD 367 (by Athanasius).[12] In AD 367, when the official list as we know it today was recognized by the church, the church was not imposing something new upon Christian communities; rather, they were codifying the documents that contained the historical beliefs and practices of those communities. Kruger explains, "The canon was like a seedling sprouting from the soil of early Christianity—although it was not fully a tree until the fourth century, it was there from the beginning."[13]

In the process of clarifying the final list of authoritative books, these Christians affirmed the church itself had been established by the words and works of Jesus as communicated by the apostles (Ephesians 2:20). Thus, the written works associated with the apostles were the objective norm by which the church was to measure and evaluate itself.[14] What gave the New Testament canon its authority is that it contained the teachings of Jesus given to the world through his apostles or those associated with the apostles.

In recognizing the canon, the early believers held that Christians, leaders, and churches were subject to the objective record of the apostles' teachings. No church body could have an authority over the Bible or equal to the Bible, as Roman Catholic and Orthodox leaders sometimes claim to have. The apostolic teaching created the church; the church did not create the Bible.[15] Clark Pinnock sums up the authority of the Bible over any church or ancient or modern form of Christianity:

THE APOSTOLIC TEACHING CREATED THE CHURCH; THE CHURCH DID NOT CREATE THE BIBLE.

> By accepting the norm of Scripture, the church declared that there was a standard outside herself to which she intended to be subject for all time. . . . The church can fall into error and needs the Bible to measure herself by. In turn, the church serves the canon by continuing in the truth and faithfully proclaiming the Word of God.[16]

The twenty-seven books of the New Testament were combined with the thirty-nine books of the Old Testament to form the canon of Scripture as the sixty-six books contained in the modern Protestant Bible.

What did we learn in this chapter? The three major steps in the process by which we received the Bible: revelation, inspiration, and canonization. We also learned the God of heaven disclosed himself and his will to the mind of human vessels who were moved by inspiration to communicate the message, and the authors wrote down the message. Finally, these messages were brought together through a canonization process of recognizing the authoritative books that circulated among God's covenant people.

REFLECTION & DISCUSSION QUESTIONS

1. What do the terms "revelation," "inspiration," and "canonization" mean?

_____

_____

_____

_____

_____

_____

2. Describe how revelation and inspiration are connected and why their connection is important.

_____

_____

_____

_____

_____

3. What are some of the ways God revealed his character in his Word?

_____

_____

_____

_____

_____

_____

_____

4. With regard to canonization, why is it significant that Jesus and his apostles continually cited and alluded to the Old Testament?

_____

_____

_____

_____

_____

_____

5. What were the three main elements the early Christians used to determine which books were authoritative and included in the Bible?

_____

_____

_____

_____

_____

_____

6. Why are you grateful that we have the Bible?

_____

_____

_____

_____

_____

_____

_____

4

HOW DO WE INTERPRET THE BIBLE?

Answer: The Bible must be read by seeking God and with an awareness of the world of the Bible and understood through observation, interpretation, and application to how we live today.

Do your best to present yourself to God as one approved, a worker who does not need to be ashamed and who correctly handles the word of truth.
— 2 Timothy 2:15

While we are grateful to have the Scriptures, it is necessary to have a process by which we can understand its meaning. Without question, the Bible requires interpretation. Like any other written communication, such as newspapers, emails, periodicals, novels, or poetry, the writings of Scripture necessitate a careful handling so the communicated message can be received.

THE BIBLE OUGHT TO BE STUDIED CAREFULLY. Moreover, it is not enough to have just any method of interpretation. Some people approach the Bible with little more than gut-level reactions and impulsive feelings as the lens through which they interpret Scripture. Others intentionally approach the Bible with prior commitments to a cultural bias. They deliberately read the Bible through this lens, which they know yields results favorable toward their chosen cause. As the Word of God, however, the Bible ought to be studied carefully—not casually or crookedly—in order to bring about authentic understanding and faithful obedience.

The field of study that approaches the task of seeking to interpret and understand the Bible is called "hermeneutics." Hermeneutics is the art and science of interpretation. It is an art because language is a form of creative expression. However, it is also a science because interpretation possesses rules that aid the reader in understanding the intent of the author. Because of the many "diverse modes of thought and ambiguities of expression" in language, hermeneutics helps remove the obstacles and bridge the gap between the author and the reader so that the reader can understand the meaning of the author.[17]

The term *hermeneutics* comes from a Greek word *hermēœneuōœ*, meaning to interpret or explain. The word is closely associated with the Greek god Hermes (known as the messenger of the gods). The word is used in the New Testament to describe the process of translation. There is a sense in which translation is in fact interpretation. This is witnessed in the three usages of the term *hermēœneuōœ* in Scripture (in italics):

> Jesus looked at him and said, "You are Simon son of John. You will be called Cephas" (which, when *translated*, is Peter). (John 1:42)

> "Go," he told him, "wash in the Pool of Siloam" (this word *means* "Sent"). So the man went and washed, and came home seeing. (John 9:7)

> First, the name Melchizedek *means* "king of righteousness"; then also, "king of Salem" *means* "king of peace." (Hebrews 7:2)

The meticulous process of translating from one language to another requires a translator to do some level of interpretation because words and expressions have a range of meaning from which to choose. The task is to choose the right term or phrase in the language of translation that reflects the original meaning of the statement. Thus, the term "hermeneutics" became the general word used for the entire process of interpretation.

WHY THE NEED FOR A PROCESS OF INTERPRETATION?

Interpretation is a part of our everyday lives. Each time we read a text message or a post on social media, we engage in the process of interpretation. Because we are familiar with how our culture communicates and the various linguistic devices we use to express thought, it is easy for us to interpret messages spoken and written in our own culture. However, interpretation can have a series of obstacles the further one is removed from the author's particular culture.

Perhaps you have gone to a foreign country and interfaced with their culture that spoke a different language and came with a different set of social norms. In order to operate and function within that cultural, you had to overcome several barriers in order to communicate with the people of that society. Several obstacles had to be removed for there to be understanding and communication. The same is true of reading an ancient document that may not reflect the values of your current culture, politics, language, or socioeconomic reality.

Even more so, when we interface with ancient documents, it can be challenging to understand what the original author was communicating in writing them because these documents came into existence in such a different time frame and culture. With this in mind, we must understand the Bible is an ancient document that reflects, or at least interacts with, a variety of cultures, religions, philosophies, languages, socioeconomic status, and politics. In order to interface with the Bible in a fruitful way, we must become more knowledgeable about these various elements so we can read God's Word as intended.

Before we discuss some of the tools for understanding the author's intended meaning, it is helpful to make one point: Is it true that a text has only one intended meaning? Couldn't Peter or Paul have intended multiple meanings when they wrote what they wrote? After all, can't a Bible verse mean something different for me than it does for you, or can't I discover a new insight from a Bible verse that I never recognized when I read it ten years ago? This is where it is helpful to introduce the distinction between "meaning" and "significance."

Meaning is what an author intended to convey by his words. You and I cannot go back and change what an author intended to convey; that's already set.

Significance, however, is a relational word.[18] Significance describes what effects and implications and relationship the text has in my life. That is, "What did the author mean to say?" is a different question from, "What is the significance of this Bible verse for my life?" Even as its significance expands throughout your life, a text of Scripture will still mean the same thing it has always meant. The meaning of a text is a matter of discovery, not innovation.

CLOSING THE DISTANCE

Since the Bible is an ancient document, there are distances we need to try to close in order to have a proper understanding of the original meaning. It is much like crossing a bridge to another world so as to understand its historical context. Thankfully, many scholars have been diligent to build bridges across these divides so modern Christians are not without resources. What are the interpretive distances that students of Scripture continue to travel in order to arrive at the meaning of a text? Let me explain five.

Time Distance. Time distance simply indicates the time between our culture today and the era in which these events happened. A significant amount of time has elapsed between current believers and the original audience. We have no access to the author nor the recipients in order to have conversations about the meaning of what they wrote or how they intended it to be received. At the very least, acknowledging this distance should give us humility to avoid impulsive, gut-level interpretations as well as curiosity to learn as much about ancient biblical history as we can. Like other "distances" we will read about in this chapter, much of the time distance can be bridged using solid resources such as Bible encyclopedias and study Bibles, which provide relevant background information for understanding the text.

Linguistic Distance. Long before our translations, such as the New American Standard Bible or the English Standard Version, the Bible was written in three ancient languages: Hebrew, Aramaic, and Koine Greek. The Old Testament was predominantly written in the Hebrew language (with some Aramaic), and the New Testament was written in Koine Greek. In an ideal world, everyone would have the ability to read such languages so this distance would be removed, but even someone who reads or speaks modern Greek and Hebrew today is still worlds apart from biblical Koine Greek and the Hebrew of the Bible. While it is certainly true that we have a plethora of reliable English translations that allow us to gain a solid understanding of biblical texts, we can still face times when some meaning is lost in the process of professional translation. To this end, it is important for serious students of the Bible, when possible and especially for teachers of the Word, to gain a basic understanding of how to use proper linguistic tools to engage with the languages of the Bible. For example, it is helpful to become familiar with lexical books to interface with these ancient languages.

Geographical Distance. The geographical distance is significant because many believers today are unfamiliar with the geographical landscape in which the events of the Bible took place. Some of the geographical terms of the Bible may be difficult to locate inasmuch as we do not have a mental picture of the landscape. Learning them, though, can aid proper interpretation.

For instance, when Jesus told the parable of the good Samaritan, he mentioned a certain man went down from Jerusalem to Jericho. What was Jesus referring to when he spoke of going down to Jericho from Jerusalem? And why would this man get robbed during the journey? A look into the geography reveals that Jericho sat about 1,500 feet below sea level, which made it much lower in elevation than Jerusalem, which was around 2,500 feet above sea level. Additionally, a look at the history of the region shows that the road from Jericho to Jerusalem was often crawling with robbers who would wait to prey upon somebody in order to steal their possessions. When Jesus spoke this parable, it would have been very plausible for the audience to picture someone traveling "down" to Jericho and getting robbed. By understanding the geography, it informs a proper understanding of the passage.

Cultural Distance. In the days of the Bible, there were various norms, customs, and ways of living that can inform a proper interpretation of Scripture. Becoming culturally informed of the norms of the biblical world can help us answer questions such as: What was so surprising about Jesus washing the feet of his disciples in John 13? Why would the apostle Paul say we should salute one another with a holy kiss in Romans 16:16? Part of understanding the cultural context of their day requires understanding their occupational world. A great many of Jesus' parables were agricultural, while others highlighted the activity of fishing. Both of these were dominant occupations within the Palestinian world.

Spiritual Distance. We have just looked at some of the prominent distances that the interpreter seeks to cross in order to arrive at a proper interpretation and fuller understanding of the text. One that I have not mentioned, however, but is the most influential divide of all, is the spiritual distance people naturally have with the Bible and the God who inspired it. If we do not humble ourselves before God and approach his Word with a willing and obedient heart, we will miss its point, even if we score A's on all the hermeneutical tests. If the Bible is the Word of God, then to study it merely out of academic pursuit or pure intellectual curiosity would be akin to taking the Lord's Supper merely for its nutritional value.

Studying the Bible with no intention of letting it bridge the spiritual distance between you and God is to prove the proverb, "Knowledge puffs up while love builds up" (1 Corinthians 8:1). Whether spoken or written, the words of God are meant to be loved (Psalm 119:97), internalized (Psalm 119:11), and obeyed (John 14:15). For this reason, it is important to read the Bible *prayerfully*, acknowledging that our study of God's Word can give rise to legalism (Luke 18:11–12) or even sinful cravings (Romans 7:7–8) if not grounded in humility before God. And a delightful surprise we experience when we do trust God enough to obey his Word is that obedience leads to understanding in a richness that study alone can never yield.

BECOMING AWARE OF GENRE

ONE CONCEPT THAT CONTRIBUTES a lot of mileage for closing the interpretive distance is genre. "Genre" in the context of biblical hermeneutics means the kind of literature of a given book of the Bible. The Bible is rich with a variety of literary genres. Being familiar with the various genres helps us read the text more accurately. For example, one of the dominant literary types in the Bible is historical narrative, such as Genesis and

Acts. The Bible also contains wisdom literature, such as Song of Solomon, Proverbs, and Ecclesiastes. There are letters written to particular church groups or individuals. Additionally, we have books containing apocalyptic literature, such as Revelation and Daniel. There are books of prophecy and law. There are sermons and parables. Moreover, poetry comprises as much as one third of the Bible.

As we each study the Bible, we must be sensitive with regard to literary genre and understand that each genre cannot be read in the exact same way. Historical narratives primarily report events, while letters address certain occasions. Wisdom literature is practical and encourages seeking virtue and divine favor, while apocalyptic contains vivid language and utilizes signs and symbols.

New Testament professor Dean Deppe provides insight to how genre affects how we read the text:

> The determination of genre is crucial to detecting the meaning of a literary text, since like an infrared lens it offers a photo that we do not always observe in normal light. . . . Genres trigger different expectations and thus demand divergent reading strategies.[19]

The goal of the interpreter is to ascertain what the author under the influence of the Holy Spirit is attempting to communicate. If we ignore the literary type, then we become vulnerable to misrepresenting the meaning. We need to read only a few words of the following description of Jesus to realize we are no longer reading a biography of Jesus in the Gospels:

> Among the lampstands was someone like a son of man, dressed in a robe reaching down to his feet and with a golden sash around his chest. The hair on his head was white like wool, as white as snow, and his eyes were like blazing fire. His feet were like bronze glowing in a furnace, and his voice was like the sound of rushing waters. (Revelation 1:13–15)

Apocalyptic literature such as we see here in Revelation 1 uses vivid imagery filled with signs and symbols.

As I mentioned, a shocking percentage of the language of Revelation comes to us from the Old Testament. Reading an unfamiliar genre (apocalypse) that borrows its imagery from the less familiar testament (the Old Testament) should invite us to tread humbly and cautiously, so as not to abuse the text. With all this in mind, how can we best understand this

IF WE IGNORE THE LITERARY TYPE, THEN WE BECOME VULNERABLE TO MISREPRESENTING THE MEANING.

apocalyptic passage undergirded with symbolism? If we take it as a literal picture of the physical description of Jesus, our interpretations could yield rather odd results. Let's walk through the text.

John describes Jesus in this text as having a robe reaching to his feet with a golden sash around his chest; his hair is white like snow and white wool; his eyes are like fire and feet like burnished bronze; and his voice is like the sound of rushing water and a two-edged sword is coming out of his mouth. Perhaps it's no wonder why Jesus needed to say in verse seventeen, "Do not be afraid."

Where do these symbols come from? The picture of Jesus dressed with a robe and sash echoes how the priests were dressed under the Old Testament law (Leviticus 16:3–4). Even more vivid is the picture of Jesus as having hair like white wool. This language recalls Daniel 7:9, where the Ancient of Days (God) is described in the same way, having his holiness placed on display. Jesus having eyes like fire recalls the language of Daniel 10:6, which reveals the image of a celestial being. His feet like bronze recalls the language of Micah 4:13, where Israel is figuratively said to have been given feet like bronze to trample out the enemy. The two-edged sword coming out of his mouth is a symbol of judgment through his word (Isaiah 49:1–2; Hebrews 4:12). His voice as rushing water is imagery of God in Ezekiel 43:1–2.

If we take all this background information under consideration and put it together with the reality that the recipients of this book were under Roman persecution needing encouragement, we arrive at something far more understandable than the incomprehensible image of Christ we started with: Christ is presented as God who is a priest to serve his people, with a sword prepared to judge, and feet that can trample out the enemy. To accent that he is God, he cites the words of Isaiah 44:6 in which Yahweh said, "I am the first and I am the last."

As this example shows, knowing the genre will help the reader handle the text accurately, according to its literary form.

THREE STEPS INVOLVED WITH UNDERSTANDING A TEXT

CULTURAL CONTEXT, GEOGRAPHICAL DISTANCE, literary genre—all of these are important considerations for interpretation. But let's take a step back from these bridge-building principles and tools and look at three broad *steps* that have long been useful in handling the Bible. This plan for handling Scripture has helped scholars, pastors, and laypeople alike approach Scripture in an accurate and faithful way. The three steps are observation, interpretation, and application. Before delving into the steps, however, let's acknowledge a posture we need to take when approaching the text: prayer. We saturate the process in prayer because our most important goal is to hear from God.

Observation is seeing what is there. It is not putting into the text something that is not there but pulling from the text that which is there. With this step we begin to know the details and answer the interrogatory questions of who, what, where, when, why, and how. These are the types of report questions we can ask of Scripture:

Who: Who is speaking? To whom is he speaking?

What: What is the subject of the text? What is the situation of the text? What is the conflict in the text? What is the solution in the text?

Where: Where are the events of this text located? Where are the original recipients located? Where is the author located?

When: What is the specified era of the text? When are these events taking place?

> **Why:** What are the reasons for some of the actions in the text? Why is the author making a particular statement? Why are the recipients responding the way they are (negatively or positively)?

> **How:** How are the recipients to accomplish the task at hand? How is the author moving the recipients to action? How did the recipients overcome the problem? How did the author overcome the problem?

Observation is the first interaction with the text. We are unlikely to arrive at a proper understanding of a text if we do not take the time to make thorough observations. The bridge-building principles we looked at earlier can help us at this stage as we try to observe everything we can about the text. However, these tools can also be helpful as we ask a more focused question: "What does this text *mean*?" This question takes us to our next step.

Interpretation moves beyond observation to getting at the meaning. This is especially where word studies and phrase studies are helpful. Words have meaning that can be determined by their context and relationships with other words. There are times when a lexicon (a foreign language dictionary) can shed light on a word's range of meaning, but it's the word's *context* that will determine the usage.

For a simple example, let's consider how the Bible defines "water." Here are two instances of the same word in the same chapter:

> When a Samaritan woman came to draw *water*, Jesus said to her, "Will you give me a drink?" . . . Jesus answered her, "If you knew the gift of God and who it is that asks you for a drink, you would have asked him and he would have given you living *water*." (John 4:7, 10)

How do we tell the difference in usage? We look at context. In John 4:7, we are meant to picture physical water. This is because the Samaritan woman was coming to a well to draw it. In John 4:10, Jesus again referred to water, but the word "living" impacts the word "water." Whatever Jesus was talking about, it's clear that it was no ordinary well water.

So how do we determine what this "living water" is referring to? For one thing, as we zoom out to the rest of the verse, we discover that it's a "gift of God." When we search the context surrounding verse ten, we discover that "living water" is connected with "eternal life" (4:14). Three chapters later, John came right out and gave the "living water" a name: "By [living water], he meant the Spirit" (7:39). What did Jesus mean by offering the woman "living water"? By seeing the context around the verse, we discover that Jesus offered her eternal life through the Holy Spirit.

In the same way, after making initial observations, we interpret what a text means by studying words and phrases in their context.

Application seeks to understand the significance of the biblical text to contemporary life. Application answers the question, "Now what?" Once the meaning of the text is understood based on the observation and interpretation, then the interpreter engages application. The interpreter should now ask questions like, "What does this passage challenge the believer to do?" and, "Is there a correlation between the circumstance of the text and the circumstance in my contemporary life?"

As we read the text, we should look to see whether each passage teaches a doctrine, exposes a false behavior, provides correction, or provides instruction in righteousness (see 2 Timothy 3:16). Perhaps your passage of choice contains a warning to heed. Take for example the warning in Hebrews 6:4–6 concerning turning away from the once-and-for-all sacrifice of Christ. Or perhaps it contains an encouragement to receive, such as that in 1 Thessalonians 4:17, when Paul wrote to reassure believers who were concerned about the Second Coming. Application itself is often a two-step process, as the reader asks, "What was this text designed to accomplish for the original hearers?" and, "How can I apply this to my present-day life?"

It is important to note that all three steps fall under the heading of "understanding a text." It is obvious that the steps of observation and interpretation are crucial in understanding a text. What may be less obvious is the role that faithfully applying the Bible to our lives plays in actually understanding it. We are missing the point—and we'll often skew the meaning—if we stop short of obeying what we read. As David Young points out, "Obedience is the best hermeneutic when it comes to the Bible."[20]

Understanding the Bible is a very important part of Christian faith. We do not display faithfulness as followers of Jesus when we flippantly read the Scriptures according to gut-level feelings or inadvertently reinterpret its texts to fit them comfortably within our cultural sensibilities. Our goal in reading Scripture is to understand what *God has revealed*. To avoid fanciful interpretations and convoluted meanings, we must prayerfully study each text in its context and utilize the bridge-building principles of observation, interpretation, and application.

REFLECTION & DISCUSSION QUESTIONS

1. Why is it important to interpret the Bible accurately?

_____

_____

_____

_____

_____

2. What are some of the lenses that you or others have used in the past that have caused you to misinterpret a passage of Scripture?

_____

_____

_____

_____

_____

_____

3. Why should we try to become familiar with elements of interpretation such as culture, history, philosophies, and languages of the original context when we seek to understand the Bible?

_____

_____

_____

_____

_____

_____

4. Of the "distances" described (time, linguistic, geographical, cultural, spiritual), which is the most difficult for you to cross when you interpret Scripture? What are some tips for helping you cross this distance?

_____

_____

_____

_____

_____

_____

5. What are the three steps this chapter describes in the study of Scripture? Can you give a brief description of each?

_____

_____

_____

_____

_____

_____

6. We must approach Scripture with humility and an obedient heart. How can you apply humility and obedience in your personal Bible study and when you disciple others?

_____

_____

_____

_____

_____

5

HOW IS THE BIBLE OUR FINAL AUTHORITY?

Answer: As the Word of God, the Bible guides our convictions and character, and, when properly understood, it has authority over all other thoughts, practices, and claims to inspiration.

All Scripture is God-breathed and is useful for teaching, rebuking, correcting and training in righteousness.
— 2 Timothy 3:16

In our brief exploration of the Bible, we have dug up too many life-altering implications to keep the information at arm's length as an object of curiosity. If the Bible is God's inspired Word, then it is true, reliable, and authoritative. And it's meant to be *our* final authority.

At Renew.org, we describe the Bible as "infallible," which means that it cannot fail in what God sets out to accomplish.[21] That is, God's Word cannot fail to communicate the truth we need about God to be saved, trained in righteousness, and transformed into the image of Jesus. It is God's uniquely inspired message to humanity that infallibly reveals God's identity, character, and will—and the path to salvation. Its purpose stands regardless of cultural winds or human weakness. We find a description of this infallibility of God's purpose in Isaiah 55:10–11:

> As the rain and the snow come down from heaven, and do not return to it without watering the earth and making it bud and flourish, so that it yields seed for the sower and bread for the eater, so is my word that goes out from my mouth: It will not return to me empty, but will accomplish what I desire and achieve the purpose for which I sent it.

So if the Bible is true, reliable, authoritative, and infallible, then each of us has a very sober question to consider: Will the Bible be *our* final authority? Of course, this doesn't mean the Bible pretends to teach everything there is to know about every subject matter. But the Bible is an authoritative set of documents that expresses God's will for our lives. Peter declares God has provided all things that pertain to "life and godliness":

> His divine power has granted to us everything pertaining to life and godliness, through the true knowledge of Him who called us by His own glory and excellence. (2 Peter 1:3, NASB)

In the immediate context of this passage, Peter encourages godly living since God has granted everything that pertains to "life and godliness." How do we receive this? It is granted "through the true knowledge of [Christ]." The term "life" as used in this context is more than likely speaking of eternal life as an abundance of life that will be fully realized in the presence

GOD'S WORD CANNOT FAIL TO COMMUNICATE THE TRUTH WE NEED ABOUT GOD TO BE SAVED.

of God. The term "godliness" refers to holy living. The Greek word for this is *eusebeia*, which expresses the idea of piety. God grants us these precious promises of life and godliness through the "true knowledge of Him who called us" (NASB), and a major way we come to this knowledge of him is through God's revelation as given through the Old and New Testaments. The gospel of Jesus is not just about forgiveness from sin; it is also for the lifelong shaping of one's character to reflect God's holiness. The implications of the Bible's claims here are as personally relevant as a claim could get.

THE AUTHORITY OF THE NEW TESTAMENT

THE GOAL OF THE New Testament is to help form our lives around Jesus Christ, in the power of the Holy Spirit, to the glory of the Father—in short, to help us to be true disciples of Jesus. So throughout the letters of the New Testament to various churches, we see several times where the writers pointed their people directly to the example of Jesus Christ. Every church struggled with weaknesses, which carried the potential to malignantly affect their church as a whole. At times, there were divisions, selfish ambitions, doctrinal disputes, or a variety of other difficulties. The authors' strategies on such occasions was often to bring the church back into Christ-centered thinking and behavior.

The Philippian church struggled with a spirit of divisiveness. In Philippians 2:1–3, the apostle Paul encourages the church to relinquish the spirit of self-centeredness and learn to honor others before themselves. In order to accent this point, Paul points to the example of Jesus:

> Have this attitude in yourselves which was also in Christ Jesus, who, as He already existed in the form of God, did not consider equality with God something to be grasped, but emptied Himself by taking the form of a bond-servant and being born in the likeness of men. And being found in appearance as a man, He humbled Himself by becoming obedient to the point of death: death on a cross. (Philippians 2:5–8, NASB)

Jesus was humble enough to empty himself of divine advantages, take on our human nature, and die a cruel and humiliating death on a cross. From looking at Jesus and his sacrifice, we see ethical values we ought to implement in our lives as believers.

The apostle Peter, similarly, in a context where suffering was a Christian's reality, highlighted the suffering of Jesus as an example to be followed. While many suffered under Nero's reign at the time of the letter, Peter encouraged the church to suffer patiently, imitating the lifestyle of their Savior. In 1 Peter 2:21–24, Peter states,

> For you have been called for this purpose, because Christ also suffered for you, leaving you an example, so that you would follow in His

steps, He who committed no sin, nor was any deceit found in His mouth; and while being abusively insulted, He did not insult in return; while suffering, He did not threaten, but kept entrusting Himself to Him who judges righteously; and He Himself brought our sins in His body up on the cross, so that we might die to sin and live for righteousness; by His wounds you were healed. (1 Peter 2:21–24, NASB)

The encouragement to suffer comes from the example of Jesus, which is an authoritative model to which Christians are to conform. So we can see the authority of the New Testament through its presentation of Jesus as a behavioral paradigm.

The Bible also presents the teaching of the apostles as authoritative for the church. Luke declares the church was devoted to the apostles' teachings (Acts 2:42). The convictions of the church are grounded in the teachings of the apostles (John 17:20). Apostleship was an authoritative position established by Jesus (Luke 6:13) in which the apostles taught truth under the direct influence of the Holy Spirit (John 14:26; 16:13). Notice how Peter views the words spoken by the apostles as the words of Jesus:

Beloved, this is now the second letter I am writing to you in which I am stirring up your sincere

> mind by way of reminder, to remember the words spoken beforehand by the holy prophets and the *commandment of the Lord and Savior spoken by your apostles.* (2 Peter 3:1–2, NASB)

In the context of this passage, where Peter encourages the church to stand against those who mock Jesus' Second Coming, he declares the church should keep in mind the words of the prophets. In concert with this admonition, the church is to also remember the words of the Savior spoken through the apostles. The apostles' teachings are to be viewed as coming from Jesus, which is a clear indication of their authoritative nature.

To briefly summarize what we've seen thus far, Jesus chose and sent out the apostles. The Holy Spirit directed them and inspired their teachings. The church devoted itself to these teachings, and when these teachings were written down, they were treated by the early Christians—as well as by fellow apostles—as inspired Scripture (e.g., see 1 Timothy 5:18; Luke 10:7; 2 Peter 3:15).

THE AUTHORITY OF THE OLD TESTAMENT

THROUGHOUT THE NEW TESTAMENT, the authors used the Old Testament as an authoritative document to substantiate their new covenant theology. Paul states the Old

Testament was written for our learning (Romans 15:4). It is important to note that during the days of the New Testament era, the canon of the Old Testament was in existence. The Old Testament was the Bible of the New Testament church while the New Testament documents were in process of being written. An excellent example of the authoritative nature of the Old Testament is that the book of Hebrews was written to prove the superiority of Jesus while using the Old Testament as authoritative evidence. Although the old covenant has been fulfilled as a system and is no longer binding—for example, animal sacrifices, temple protocols, Israel's national regulations—the Old Testament is still an authoritative document that supports foundational Christian doctrine.

THE OLD TESTAMENT WAS WRITTEN FOR OUR LEARNING.

I already mentioned how Hebrews accentuates the supremacy of Jesus, but notice how the author uses arguments from the Old Testament to present Jesus' superiority:

> For to which of the angels did God ever say, "You are my Son; today I have become your Father"? Or again, "I will be his Father, and he will be my Son"? And again, when God brings his firstborn into the world, he says, "Let all God's angels

worship him." In speaking of the angels he says, "He makes his angels spirits, and his servants flames of fire." But about the Son he says, "Your throne, O God, will last for ever and ever; a scepter of justice will be the scepter of your kingdom. You have loved righteousness and hated wickedness; therefore God, your God, has set you above your companions by anointing you with the oil of joy." He also says, "In the beginning, Lord, you laid the foundations of the earth, and the heavens are the work of your hands. They will perish, but you remain; they will all wear out like a garment. You will roll them up like a robe; like a garment they will be changed. But you remain the same, and your years will never end." To which of the angels did God ever say, "Sit at my right hand until I make your enemies a footstool for your feet"? Are not all angels ministering spirits sent to serve those who will inherit salvation? (Hebrews 1:5–14)

The Hebrew writer cites several passages to substantiate his position regarding Christ, such as Psalm 2:7, one of the royal psalms used for the inauguration of a king. This passage acknowledges Jesus as being not only the Son of God but also the *appointed Son*, who now reigns over his kingdom. Then, the author provides a loose quotation of Psalm 104:4 to contrast the angels to God's

Son. To accent the superiority of Jesus, the author quotes Psalm 45:6–7, attributing divinity to Jesus Christ. While in the original context, the psalmists praised God for his greatness, the writer of Hebrews interprets the passage as an exclamation of God to his Son. In essence, God referred to his Son as God, proclaiming he would reign forever and ever. The author goes as far as to cite Psalm 102:25–26 to acknowledge Jesus was at work creating the world in Genesis 1.

Clearly, the Bible is an authoritative charter for the church as it presents Christ as the quintessential model for living and the object of Christian faith. That authority is also manifested through the authoritative word of the apostles and undergirded by Old Testament revelation. Its authority over the people of God means we subject our lifestyles to its norms (2 Timothy 3:16–17); we submit our thoughts to its truth (Mark 12:24); we surrender our practices to its commands (Mark 7:13); and we reject all other claims to inspiration that defy the once-for-all faith that has been entrusted to us (Jude 1:3; Galatians 1:7–9).

Thus, we return to the central question of this chapter: How is the Bible *our* final authority? After having explored ways in which the Bible exercises authority for the people of God, perhaps the best way to answer the question personally is with another question: How much do you truly trust Jesus? Part of trusting Jesus this side of heaven means to follow his teachings. For Jesus, how we treat the Bible is a relational question more than an intellectual or even ethical one. For Jesus told his disciples, "If you love me, keep my commands" (John 14:15).

Culture will often challenge the authority of the Word of God. Paul speaks to this:

> The time will come when people will not put up with sound doctrine. Instead, to suit their own desires, they will gather around them a great number of teachers to say what their itching ears want to hear. They will turn their ears away from the truth and turn aside to myths. (2 Timothy 4:3–4)

Whichever way worldly cultures might drift, the authority for a disciple of Jesus remains clear, as Paul tells Timothy a handful of verses earlier: "All Scripture is God-breathed and is useful for teaching, rebuking, correcting and training in righteousness" (2 Timothy 3:16).

There will be days when we don't feel like trusting Jesus by following his teachings. This will be a good time to remind ourselves that trees do not derive their health from their impressive branches or fancy foliage but from being connected to their source. As the psalmist writes:

> Blessed is the one . . . whose delight is in the law of the Lord, and who meditates on his law day

and night. That person is like a tree planted by streams of water, which yields its fruit in season and whose leaf does not wither—whatever they do prospers. . . . For the LORD watches over the way of the righteous, but the way of the wicked leads to destruction. (Psalm 1:1–3, 6)

On dark and confusing days, you can know the direction to take because God's Word is a "lamp for [your] feet, a light on [your] path" (Psalm 119:105). Praise God that you have "the prophetic message as something completely reliable, and you will do well to pay attention to it, as to a light shining in a dark place, until the day dawns and the morning star rises in your hearts" (2 Peter 1:19).

God has spoken. May we be a faithful people who listen and trust and follow.

REFLECTION & DISCUSSION QUESTIONS

1. What does it mean to say the Bible is "infallible"?

_____

_____

_____

_____

_____

2. What Scriptures point to the authority of the apostles' teaching?

_____

_____

_____

_____

_____

_____

3. In your own words, describe the goal of the New Testament.

_____

_____

_____

_____

_____

_____

4. Does the Old Testament still carry authority in our lives as disciples of Jesus? If so, in what ways does it?

_____

_____

_____

_____

_____

_____

_____

5. How does the authority of Scripture influence our daily lives? Give specific examples.

_____

_____

_____

_____

_____

_____

6. How would you describe to a non-believer why you believe in the authority of Scripture?

_____

_____

_____

_____

_____

_____

_____

APPENDIX A

BOOK RECOMMENDATIONS FOR FURTHER STUDY

Craig Blomberg, *Can We Still Believe the Bible? An Evangelical Engagement with Contemporary Questions* (Grand Rapids: Brazos Press, 2014).

F. F. Bruce, *The Canon of Scripture* (Downers Grove, IL: InterVarsity Press, 1988).

Kevin DeYoung, *Taking God at His Word* (Wheaton, IL: Crossway, 2014).

John Frame, *The Doctrine of the Word of God* (Phillipsburg, NJ: P&R, 2010).

Michael Kruger, *The Question of Canon: Challenging the Status Quo in the New Testament Debate* (Downers Grove, IL: InterVarsity Press, 2013).

Michael Kruger, *The Canon Revisited: Establishing the Origins and Authority of the New Testament Books* (Wheaton, IL: Crossway, 2012).

Anthony N. S. Lane, "Sola Scriptura? Making Sense of a Post-Reformation Slogan," in *A Pathway into the Holy Scripture*, ed. Philip Satterthwaite and David Wright (Grand Rapids: Eerdmans, 1994).

Bruce M. Metzger, *The Canon of the New Testament* (Oxford: Oxford University Press, 1987).

APPENDIX B

Mission: We Renew the Teachings of Jesus to Fuel Disciple Making

Vision: A collaborative network equipping millions of disciples, disciple makers, and church planters among all ethnicities.

SEVEN VALUES

RENEWAL IN THE BIBLE and in history follows a discernible outline that can be summarized by seven key elements. We champion these elements as our core values. They are listed in a sequential pattern that is typical of renewal, and it all starts with God.

1. *Renewing by God's Spirit.* We believe that God is the author of renewal and that he invites us to access and join him through prayer and fasting for the Holy Spirit's work of renewal.
2. *Following God's Word.* We learn the ways of God with lasting clarity and conviction by trusting God's Word and what it teaches as the objective foundation for renewal and life.
3. *Surrendering to Jesus' Lordship.* The gospel teaches us that Jesus is Messiah (King) and Lord. He calls everyone to salvation (in eternity) and discipleship (in this life) through a faith commitment that is expressed in repentance, confession, and baptism. Repentance and surrender to Jesus as Lord is the never-ending cycle for life in Jesus' kingdom, and it is empowered by the Spirit.
4. *Championing disciple making.* Jesus personally gave us his model of disciple making, which he demonstrated with his disciples. Those same principles from the life of Jesus should be utilized as we make disciples today and champion discipleship as the core mission of the local church.
5. *Loving like Jesus.* Jesus showed us the true meaning of love and taught us that sacrificial love is the

distinguishing character trait of true disciples (and true renewal). Sacrificial love is the foundation for our relationships both in the church and in the world.

6. *Living in holiness.* Just as Jesus lived differently from the world, the people in his church will learn to live differently than the world. Even when it is difficult, we show that God's kingdom is an alternative kingdom to the world.

7. *Leading courageously.* God always uses leaders in renewal who live by a prayerful, risk-taking faith. Renewal will be led by bold and courageous leaders—who make disciples, plant churches, and create disciple making movements.

TEN FAITH STATEMENTS

WE BELIEVE THAT JESUS Christ is Lord. We are a group of church leaders inviting others to join the theological and disciple making journey described below. We want to trust and follow Jesus Christ to the glory of God the Father in the power of the Holy Spirit. We are committed to *restoring* the kingdom vision of Jesus and the apostles, especially the *message* of Jesus' gospel, the *method* of disciple making he showed us, and the *model* of what a community of his disciples, at their best, can become.

We live in a time when cultural pressures are forcing us to face numerous difficulties and complexities in following God. Many are losing their resolve. We trust that God is gracious and forgives the errors of those with genuine faith in his Son, but our desire is to be faithful in all things.

Our focus is disciple making, which is both reaching lost people (evangelism) and bringing people to maturity (sanctification). We seek to be a movement of disciple making leaders who make disciples and other disciple makers. We want to renew existing churches and help plant multiplying churches.

1. *God's Word.* We believe God gave us the sixty-six books of the Bible to be received as the inspired, authoritative, and infallible Word of God for salvation and life. The documents of Scripture come to us as diverse literary and historical writings. Despite their complexities, they can be understood, trusted, and followed. We want to do the hard work of wrestling to understand Scripture in order to obey God. We want to avoid the errors of interpreting Scripture through the sentimental lens of our feelings and opinions or through a complex re-interpretation of plain meanings so that the Bible says what our culture says. Ours is a time for both clear thinking and courage. Because the Holy Spirit inspired all sixty-six books, we honor Jesus' Lordship by submitting our lives to all that God has for us in them.

Psalm 1; 119; Deuteronomy 4:1–6; 6:1–9;
2 Chronicles 34; Nehemiah 8; Matthew 5:1–7:28;
15:6–9; John 12:44–50; Matthew 28:19; Acts 2:42;
17:10–11; 2 Timothy 3:16–4:4; 1 Peter 1:20–21.

2. *Christian convictions.* We believe the Scriptures reveal three distinct elements of the faith: *essential* elements which are necessary for salvation; *important* elements which are to be pursued so that we faithfully follow Christ; and *personal* elements or opinion. The gospel is *essential.* Every person who is indwelt and sealed by God's Holy Spirit because of their faith in the gospel is a brother or a sister in Christ. *Important* but secondary elements of the faith are vital. Our faithfulness to God requires us to seek and pursue them, even as we acknowledge that our salvation may not be dependent on getting them right. And thirdly, there are personal matters of opinion, disputable areas where God gives us personal freedom. But we are never at liberty to express our freedom in a way that causes others to stumble in sin. In all things, we want to show understanding, kindness, and love.

1 Corinthians 15:1–8; Romans 1:15–17;
Galatians 1:6–9; 2 Timothy 2:8; Ephesians 1:13–14;
4:4–6; Romans 8:9; 1 Corinthians 12:13;
1 Timothy 4:16; 2 Timothy 3:16–4:4;

Matthew 15:6–9; Acts 20:32; 1 Corinthians 11:1–2; 1 John 2:3–4; 2 Peter 3:14–16; Romans 14:1–23.

3. *The gospel.* We believe God created all things and made human beings in his image, so that we could enjoy a relationship with him and each other. But we lost our way, through Satan's influence. We are now spiritually dead, separated from God. Without his help, we gravitate toward sin and self-rule. The gospel is God's good news of reconciliation. It was promised to Abraham and David and revealed in Jesus' life, ministry, teaching, and sacrificial death on the cross. The gospel is the saving action of the triune God. The Father sent the Son into the world to take on human flesh and redeem us. Jesus came as the promised Messiah of the Old Testament. He ushered in the kingdom of God, died for our sins according to Scripture, was buried, and was raised on the third day. He defeated sin and death and ascended to heaven. He is seated at the right hand of God as Lord and he is coming back for his disciples. Through the Spirit, we are transformed and sanctified. God will raise everyone for the final judgment. Those who trusted and followed Jesus by faith will not experience punishment for their sins and separation from God in hell. Instead, we will join together with God in the renewal of all things in the consummated kingdom. We will live

together in the new heaven and new earth where we will glorify God and enjoy him forever.

> *Genesis 1–3; Romans 3:10–12; 7:8–25;*
> *Genesis 12:1–3; Galatians 3:6–9; Isaiah 11:1–4;*
> *2 Samuel 7:1–16; Micah 5:2–4; Daniel 2:44–45;*
> *Luke 1:33; John 1:1–3; Matthew 4:17;*
> *1 Corinthians 15:1–8; Acts 1:11; 2:36; 3:19–21;*
> *Colossians 3:1; Matthew 25:31–32; Revelation 21:1ff;*
> *Romans 3:21–26.*

4. *Faithful faith.* We believe that people are saved by grace through faith. The gospel of Jesus' kingdom calls people to both salvation and discipleship—no exceptions, no excuses. Faith is more than mere intellectual agreement or emotional warmth toward God. It is living and active; faith is surrendering our self-rule to the rule of God through Jesus in the power of the Spirit. We surrender by trusting and following Jesus as both Savior and Lord in all things. Faith includes allegiance, loyalty, and faithfulness to him.

> *Ephesians 2:8–9; Mark 8:34–38; Luke 14:25–35;*
> *Romans 1:3, 5; 16:25–26; Galatians 2:20;*
> *James 2:14–26; Matthew 7:21–23; Galatians 4:19;*
> *Matthew 28:19–20; 2 Corinthians 3:3, 17–18;*
> *Colossians 1:28.*

5. *New birth.* God so loved the world that he gave his one and only Son, that whoever believes in him shall not perish but have eternal life. To believe in Jesus means we trust and follow him as both Savior and Lord. When we commit to trust and follow Jesus, we express this faith by repenting from sin, confessing his name, and receiving baptism by immersion in water. Baptism, as an expression of faith, is for the remission of sins. We uphold baptism as the normative means of entry into the life of discipleship. It marks our commitment to regularly die to ourselves and rise to live for Christ in the power of the Holy Spirit. We believe God sovereignly saves as he sees fit, but we are bound by Scripture to uphold this teaching about surrendering to Jesus in faith through repentance, confession, and baptism.

> *1 Corinthians 8:6; John 3:1–9; 3:16–18;*
> *3:19–21; Luke 13:3–5; 24:46–47; Acts 2:38;*
> *3:19; 8:36–38; 16:31–33; 17:30; 20:21; 22:16;*
> *26:20; Galatians 3:26–27; Romans 6:1–4;*
> *10:9–10; 1 Peter 3:21; Romans 2:25–29;*
> *2 Chronicles 30:17–19; Matthew 28:19–20;*
> *Galatians 2:20; Acts 18:24–26.*

6. *Holy Spirit.* We believe God's desire is for everyone to be saved and come to the knowledge of the truth. Many hear the gospel but do not believe it because they

are blinded by Satan and resist the pull of the Holy Spirit. We encourage everyone to listen to the Word and let the Holy Spirit convict them of their sin and draw them into a relationship with God through Jesus. We believe that when we are born again and indwelt by the Holy Spirit, we are to live as people who are filled, empowered, and led by the Holy Spirit. This is how we walk with God and discern his voice. A prayerful life, rich in the Holy Spirit, is fundamental to true discipleship and living in step with the kingdom reign of Jesus. We seek to be a prayerful, Spirit-led fellowship.

> *1 Timothy 2:4; John 16:7–11; Acts 7:51;*
> *1 John 2:20, 27; John 3:5; Ephesians 1:13–14;*
> *5:18; Galatians 5:16–25; Romans 8:5–11;*
> *Acts 1:14; 2:42; 6:6; 9:40; 12:5; 13:3; 14:23; 20:36;*
> *2 Corinthians 3:3.*

7. Disciple making. We believe the core mission of the local church is making disciples of Jesus Christ—it is God's plan "A" to redeem the world and manifest the reign of his kingdom. We want to be disciples who make disciples because of our love for God and others. We personally seek to become more and more like Jesus through his Spirit so that Jesus would live through us. To help us focus on Jesus, his sacrifice on the cross, our unity in him, and his coming return, we typically share communion in our weekly gatherings. We desire the fruits of biblical disciple making which are disciples who live and love like Jesus and "go" into every corner of society and to the ends of the earth. Disciple making is the engine that drives our missional service to those outside the church. We seek to be known where we live for the good that we do in our communities. We love and serve all people, as Jesus did, no strings attached. At the same time, as we do good for others, we also seek to form relational bridges that we prayerfully hope will open doors for teaching people the gospel of the kingdom and the way of salvation.

> *Matthew 28:19–20; Galatians 4:19;*
> *Acts 2:41; Philippians 1:20–21; Colossians 1:27–29;*
> *2 Corinthians 3:3; 1 Thessalonians 2:19–20;*
> *John 13:34–35; 1 John 3:16; 1 Corinthians 13:1–13;*
> *Luke 22:14–23; 1 Corinthians 11:17–24; Acts 20:7.*

8. *Kingdom life.* We believe in the present kingdom reign of God, the power of the Holy Spirit to transform people, and the priority of the local church. God's holiness should lead our churches to reject lifestyles characterized by pride, sexual immorality, homosexuality, easy divorce, idolatry, greed, materialism, gossip, slander, racism, violence, and the like. God's love should lead our churches to emphasize love as the distinguishing sign of

a true disciple. Love for one another should make the church like an extended family—a fellowship of married people, singles, elderly, and children who are all brothers and sisters to one another. The love of the extended church family to one another is vitally important. Love should be expressed in both service to the church and to the surrounding community. It leads to the breaking down of walls (racial, social, political), evangelism, acts of mercy, compassion, forgiveness, and the like. By demonstrating the ways of Jesus, the church reveals God's kingdom reign to the watching world.

> *1 Corinthians 1:2; Galatians 5:19–21;*
> *Ephesians 5:3–7; Colossians 3:5–9;*
> *Matthew 19:3–12; Romans 1:26–32; 14:17–18;*
> *1 Peter 1:15–16; Matthew 25:31–46;*
> *John 13:34–35; Colossians 3:12–13; 1 John 3:16;*
> *1 Corinthians 13:1–13; 2 Corinthians 5:16–21.*

9. *Counter-cultural living.* We believe Jesus' Lordship through Scripture will lead us to be a distinct light in the world. We follow the first and second Great Commandments where love and loyalty to God come first and love for others comes second. So we prioritize the gospel and one's relationship with God, with a strong commitment to love people in their secondary points of need too. The gospel is God's light for us. It teaches us

grace, mercy, and love. It also teaches us God's holiness, justice, and the reality of hell which led to Jesus' sacrifice of atonement for us. God's light is grace and truth, mercy and righteousness, love and holiness. God's light among us should be reflected in distinctive ways like the following:

A. We believe that human life begins at conception and ends upon natural death, and that all human life is priceless in the eyes of God. All humans should be treated as image-bearers of God. For this reason, we stand for the sanctity of life both at its beginning and its end. We oppose elective abortions and euthanasia as immoral and sinful. We understand that there are very rare circumstances that may lead to difficult choices when a mother or child's life is at stake, and we prayerfully surrender and defer to God's wisdom, grace, and mercy in those circumstances.

B. We believe God created marriage as the context for the expression and enjoyment of sexual relations. Jesus defines marriage as a covenant between one man and one woman. We believe that all sexual activity outside the bounds of marriage, including same-sex unions and same-sex marriage, are immoral and must not be condoned by disciples of Jesus.

C. We believe that Jesus invites all races and ethnicities into the kingdom of God. Because humanity has exhibited grave racial injustices throughout history, we believe that everyone, especially disciples, must be proactive in securing justice for people of all races and that racial reconciliation must be a priority for the church.

D. We believe that both men and women were created by God to equally reflect, in gendered ways, the nature and character of God in the world. In marriage, husbands and wives are to submit to one another, yet there are gender specific expressions: husbands model themselves in relationship with their wives after Jesus' sacrificial love for the church, and wives model themselves in relationship with their husbands after the church's willingness to follow Jesus. In the church, men and women serve as partners in the use of their gifts in ministry, while seeking to uphold New Testament norms which teach that the lead teacher/preacher role in the gathered church and the elder/overseer role are for qualified men. The vision of the Bible is an equal partnership of men and women in creation, in marriage, in salvation, in the gifts of the Spirit, and in the ministries of the church but exercised in ways that honor gender as described in the Bible.

E. We believe that we must resist the forces of culture that focus on materialism and greed. The Bible teaches that the love of money is the root of all sorts of evil and that greed is idolatry. Disciples of Jesus should joyfully give liberally and work sacrificially for the poor, the marginalized, and the oppressed.

Romans 12:3–8; Matthew 22:36–40; 1 Corinthians 12:4–7; Ephesians 2:10; 4:11–13; 1 Peter 4:10–11; Matthew 20:24–27; Philippians 1:1; Acts 20:28; 1 Timothy 2:11–15; 3:1–7; Titus 1:5–9; 1 Corinthians 11:2–9; 14:33–36; Ephesians 5:21–33; Colossians 3:18–19; 1 Corinthians 7:32–35.

10. *The end.* We believe that Jesus is coming back to earth in order to bring this age to an end. Jesus will reward the saved and punish the wicked, and finally destroy God's last enemy, death. He will put all things under the Father, so that God may be all in all forever. That is why we have urgency for the Great Commission—to make disciples of all nations. We like to look at the Great Commission as an inherent part of God's original command to "be fruitful and multiply."

We want to be disciples of Jesus who love people and help them to be disciples of Jesus. We are a movement of disciples who make disciples who help renew existing churches and who start new churches that make more disciples. We want to reach as many as possible—until Jesus returns and God restores all creation to himself in the new heaven and new earth.

Matthew 25:31–32; Acts 17:31; Revelation 20:11–15; 2 Thessalonians 1:6–10; Mark 9:43–49; Luke 12:4–7; Acts 4:12; John 14:6; Luke 24:46–48; Matthew 28:19–20; Genesis 12:1–3; Galatians 2:20; 4:19; Luke 6:40; Luke 19:10; Revelation 21:1ff.

APPENDIX C

THE APOCRYPHA

I s it possible that there were mant to be more than six-ty-six books in the Bible? There are additional books that are considered by Roman Catholic and Eastern Orthodox Churches to be part of the biblical canon. In this appendix, we will briefly explore the Apocrypha and ask whether these additional books were meant to belong in the Bible.

Although all Christians accept the sixty-six books of the Old and New Testaments as authoritative, Roman Catholic and Eastern Orthodox Churches include additional books sometimes called "deuterocanonical" or "apocryphal" books. These additional books were included in the Greek translation of the Hebrew Bible (the Septuagint) and subsequently adopted by some Christians as authoritative. They include the books of Tobit, Judith, 1 and 2 Maccabees, the Wisdom of

Solomon, Ecclesiasticus, Baruch, and additional por-
tions of Daniel and Esther.

Although these books are accepted within Catholic
and Eastern Orthodox traditions as canonical, they
are not seen as authoritative by Protestant traditions.
A major reason Protestants reject the canonicity of the
Apocrypha is that these books were not part of the
Hebrew canon and were not part of the authoritative
Hebrew and Aramaic text known as the Masoretic
Text. Similarly, the Apocrypha was not included in
first-century Jewish historian Josephus's description of
the Hebrew canon.[22]

What was the Apocrypha's relationship with the
New Testament? None of the apocryphal books were
directly quoted in the writings of the New Testament
as authoritative. This is in contrast to the many Old
Testament quotations throughout the New Testament.
However, the New Testament does include allusions to
apocryphal writing.

While we do not consider these books to be canonical, they still hold value. For example, they can provide historical and reliable snapshots of faithfulness to
God during difficult times. The stories of a Jewish family that helped restore the nation between the Seleucid
and Roman takeovers are fascinating and provide valuable background information to understand the New
Testament world. We can read these stories in the

apocryphal books of 1 and 2 Maccabees. But while they are valuable, we must not put the apocryphal books on the same level as inspired Scripture. Fifth-century church father Jerome articulated a helpful perspective on the Apocrypha with a similar sentiment: "These are books that, though not esteemed like the Holy Scriptures, are still both useful and good to read."[23]

Throughout church history there had been voices, such as Augustine's, arguing for the full canonicity of the apocryphal books, but it was not until after the Protestant Reformation that this became official Roman Catholic doctrine. The Roman Catholic Church made acceptance of these books their official position at the Council of Trent in reaction to the Protestant Reformation. The question of the Apocrypha's canonicity is not insignificant for church doctrine because some of the apocryphal books have been used to substantiate doctrines that are not explicitly taught in either the Old Testament or New Testament. These include prayers for the dead, the worship of angels, the veneration of saints, purgatory, and the sale of indulgences—issues which Protestants and Catholics have historically disagreed over.

Here is a list of reasons why we recommend treating the Apocrypha as mere historical documents and not as Scripture:

1. They were written in the intertestamental times, after the Old Testament canon was closed.
2. The Jews rejected the Apocrypha as part of the Old Testament canon in the time of Jesus and afterward. It was part of the Greek translation of the Old Testament called the Septuagint, but not part of the Hebrew translation called the Masoretic Text.
3. Jesus Christ and the apostles never directly quoted from them or cited them as Scripture, even though there are some allusions to apocryphal writings.
4. They contain historical problems and contradictions regarding doctrinal teachings taught elsewhere in the Bible.
5. After centuries of debate, the Apocrypha was officially included as authoritative Scripture for the Roman Catholic Church in the 1500s, and it was in response to the rise of Protestantism.

NOTES

1. The alteration to this three-fold division was in part due to the Scriptures' being written in Greek (e.g., the Septuagint), which organized the books according to literary type of law, history, poetry, and prophecy. Julius Scott Jr. explains the shift from the traditional threefold division into a more topical organization: "The advent of Hellenism and the subsequent appearance of the Scriptures in Greek brought a challenge to the consensus. The books in the Septuagint, other than the five of Moses, were arranged according to literary types. This undermined the threefold division and its implications for interpretation." See Julius Scott Jr., *Jewish Backgrounds of the New Testament* (Grand Rapids: Baker Academic, 2000), 138.

2. Rachel Klippenstein and J. David Stark, ed. John D. Barry et al., *The Lexham Bible Dictionary* (Bellingham, WA: Lexham Press, 2016), s.v. "New Testament."

3. Craig S. Keener, *Christobiography: Memory, History, and Reliability of the Gospels* (Grand Rapids: Eerdmans, 2019), 1.

4. See Josephus, "Josephus on James" in *Antiquities,* book 20, chap. 9, https://pages.uncc.edu/james-tabor/ancient-judaism/josephus-james/, and Philip Schaff, *Nicene and Post-Nicene Fathers,* ser. 2, vol. 1, chap. 25, https://www.ccel.org/ccel/schaff/npnf201.iii.vii.xxvi.html.

5. For more on the end of history, see Gary L. Johnson, *The End: The Return of King Jesus and the Renewal of All Things* (Renew.org, 2021).

6. For more detailed information about what follows, consult the seminal works of F. F. Bruce, *The Canon of Scripture* (Downers Grove, IL: InterVarsity Press, 1988), and Bruce M. Metzger, *The Canon of the New Testament* (Oxford: Oxford University Press, 1987).

7. David Noel Freedman, ed., *The Anchor Bible Dictionary* (New York: Doubleday, 1992), s.v. "canon."

8. David A. deSilva, *An Introduction to the New Testament: Contexts, Methods & Ministry Formation,* 2nd ed. (Downers Grove, IL: IVP Academic, 2018).

9. Michael J. Kruger, *The Question of Canon: Challenging the Status Quo in the New Testament Debate* (Downers Grove, IL: InterVarsity Press, 2013), 206.

10. Michael J. Kruger, *Canon Revisited: Establishing the Origins and Authority of the New Testament Books* (Wheaton, IL: Crossway, 2012), 292.

11. See Bruce M. Metzger, *The Canon of the New Testament* (Oxford: Oxford University Press, 1987).

12. Michael J. Kruger, "10 Misconceptions About the NT Canon: #10: 'Athanasius' Festal Letter (367 A.D.) Is the First Complete List of New Testament Books,'" December 11, 2012, accessed January 19, 2021, https://www.michaeljkruger.com/10-misconceptions-about-the-nt-canon-10-athanasius-festal-letter-367-a-d-is-the-first-complete-list-of-new-testament-books/.

13. Michael Kruger, *The Question of Canon*, 210.

14. This is an important fact that is in contradistinction to the claims of the Roman Catholic Church as definitively stated by Oscar Cullman in the advanced debates leading up to Vatican II; see "The Tradition," in *The Early Church* (London: SCM Press, 1956).

15. Kruger, *The Question of Canon,* 91.

16. Clark H. Pinnock, *The Scripture Principle* (Vancouver: Regent College Publishing, 1984), 81–82.

17. Milton S. Terry, *Biblical Hermeneutics: A Treatise on the Interpretation of the Old and New Testaments,* ed. George R. Crooks and John F. Hurst, New Edition, Thoroughly Revised, vol. 2, Library of Biblical and Theological Literature (New York; Cincinnati: Eaton & Mains; Curts & Jennings, 1890), 17.

18. For the difference between meaning and significance, see E. D. Hirsch, *Validity in Interpretation* (New Haven: Yale University Press, 1967), 8.

19. Dean B. Deppe, *All Roads Lead to the Text: Eight Methods of Inquiry into the Bible* (Grand Rapids: Eerdmans, 2011), 7.

20. David Young, *A Grand Illusion: How Progressive Christianity Undermines Biblical Faith* (Renew.org, 2019), 72.

21. For more on Renew.org's understanding of infallibility, see I. Howard Marshall, *Biblical Inspiration* (Vancouver: Regent College Publications, 2004).

22. To read Josephus's description of the Hebrew canon as well as a helpful commentary on it, see "Josephus: Historical Evidence of the Old Testament Canon," *Blue Letter Bible,* May 29, 2012, accessed July 26, 2021, https://blogs.blueletterbible.org/blb/2012/05/29/josephus-historical-evidence-of-the-old-testament-canon/.

23. David E. Briones, "A Brief History of the Apocrypha," November 6, 2019, accessed January 19, 2021, https://faculty.wts.edu/posts/a-brief-history-of-the-apocrypha/.